A THEATRE *History of* MARION OHIO

JOHN EBERSON'S PALACE & BEYOND

Scott L. Hoffman

I0792619

THE History PRESS

Published by The History Press
Charleston, SC 29403
www.historypress.net

Copyright © 2015 by Scott L. Hoffman
All rights reserved

Cover image © Lew Lause. Used by permission.

First published 2015

Manufactured in the United States

ISBN 978.1.62619.950.7

Library of Congress Control Number: 2014957209

Notice: The information in this book is true and complete to the best of our knowledge. It is offered without guarantee on the part of the author or The History Press. The author and The History Press disclaim all liability in connection with the use of this book.

All rights reserved. No part of this book may be reproduced or transmitted in any form whatsoever without prior written permission from the publisher except in the case of brief quotations embodied in critical articles and reviews.

Dedicated to all of the members of the Palace Cultural Arts Association, past and present, who with steady persistence overcame difficulties, obstacles and sometimes discouragement to preserve a Marion landmark.

CONTENTS

CONTENTS

ACKNOWLEDGEMENTS

I am indebted to several collectors of Marion, Ohio postcards, photographs and artifacts who kindly helped me in preparing this book.

Randy Winland, author of *Marion* in the Arcadia Publishing Postcard History Series, opened his home and extensive collection to me and provided comments on an early version of the manuscript. He also lightened my workload by guiding research for me at the Marion County Historical Society. I benefited from his extensive knowledge and thoughtful comments about Marion history.

Mike Perry also opened his home and equally extensive collection to me. His personal collection of theatre photographs and programs was particularly helpful to me in researching the other theatres of Marion.

The Marion County Historical Society and the Palace Cultural Arts Association each generously made their archives available to me, and I am grateful for their help. These are excellent organizations and deserve our support. If you are not a member, I encourage you to join.

Finally, I am grateful to Lew Lause, photographer, whose images of the Marion Palace Theatre capture both the beauty of the Marion Palace Theatre and the spirit of John Eberson's creativity.

INTRODUCTION

Motion picture palaces were buildings of escape, fantasy and illusion—unique architectural reflections of America in the 1920s. They were gaudy and ornate yet comfortable and approachable. They were aristocratic in name and design yet egalitarian in use. They were opulently decorated yet designed for commercial use. They used modern theatre equipment yet hid it behind a contrived façade of antiquity. Most significantly, they were an expression of the pervasive consumerism that occurred in the 1920s, an ideology that permanently altered the way Americans lived and interacted with the world.

Exhausted by the human losses of World War I and the tragedy of the Spanish flu epidemic, Americans hungered for "normalcy"—a term coined by Warren G. Harding. The entertainment business was happy to oblige. While vaudeville had been on a slow decline since the early 1910s, the silent motion picture business was booming. With the advent of the feature-length film, Americans were no longer willing to be entertained while seated on hard wooden chairs in poorly ventilated, family-owned storefront nickelodeons. The motion picture palaces provided the comfort patrons wanted, each with 1,500 to 3,000 seats or more to satisfy growing demand.

That demand seemed almost insatiable. Newspapers fed the appetite with stories about new productions and the gossip about movie stars. Americans bought tickets for pictures featuring swashbuckler, horror and romantic comedy themes. Douglas Fairbanks, Greta Garbo, Mary Pickford, Lillian Gish, Charlie Chaplin, Buster Keaton, Clara Bow, Gloria

Swanson, Joan Crawford and John Barrymore were as well known then as movie stars of today.

But it was not professional theatre. Some Americans were still conservative enough to raise an eyebrow about motion pictures. They were still associated in the popular mind with dark nickelodeons and risqué vaudeville. Neither satisfied the highbrow definition of "legitimate" theatre. Motion pictures were simply not serious.

The motion picture palace provided that legitimacy. In one respectable building, architects made space for motion pictures, live orchestra music, organ music, stage productions and family-oriented vaudeville. Patrons of all walks of life could be culturally comfortable in these buildings, without fear of criticism for attending.

The Marion Palace Theatre—a motion picture palace—fit exactly into this formula. It was designed for theatre productions, motion pictures and vaudeville. The stage could accommodate large productions, and the pit was designed for a small orchestra. The auditorium was spacious, well ventilated and fitted with comfortable leather seats.

Architecturally, it was a marked departure from earlier theatres. Rather than an ornate box, it was designed as an atmospheric theatre, in this case a palace on the exterior and a courtyard on the inside. Reproductions of famous Greek and Roman statues placed in niches and balconies throughout the auditorium created a sense of culture and refinement. A statue of George Washington, guarding the balcony, reassured patrons that the theatre was as legitimate as the country.

An added benefit of the atmospheric style of a motion picture palace was the sense of immersion that it provided. Theatre patrons bought not only a ticket for entertainment but also a ticket to enter another world. Like the motion pictures they watched on the screen, the Marion Palace interior was exotic, romantic and melodramatic. The patrons often described that they felt part of the motion picture, enveloped by both the screen and the interior.

For the thirty thousand residents of Marion, the Palace continued the city's transformation from a dusty manufacturing town to a well-known, modern city with a new hotel, interurban rail transportation and an enviable industrial rail system. Money was plentiful among the nouveau riche industrialists who made Marion their home. Plentiful also were the political contacts citizens made during the presidency of Warren G. Harding, who lived in Marion during his adult life. What it lacked was a modern, permanent home for a cultural life. The Marion Palace provided it, and the entire city gushed with delight on August 30, 1928, its opening night.

INTRODUCTION

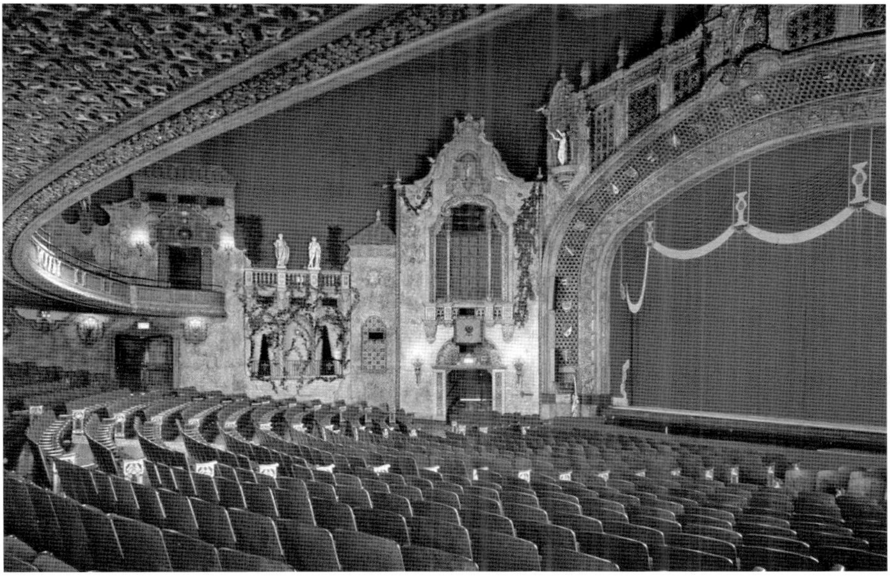

The interior of the Marion Palace Theatre today. View from the orchestra section that is under the balcony. *Courtesy of Lew Lause. ©Lew Lause.*

Even as the Palace opened, entertainment had changed. Designed for "talkies," the Palace had to open with a silent motion picture because the needed equipment for sound motion pictures had not arrived. The success of talkies, a new technology only two years before, had been widely successful. Vaudeville could not compete, and its own stars contributed to the demise of its popularity as they recorded their acts on film, resulting in no demand to see live acts that had already been seen on film.

Before the end of the decade, the Great Depression would shatter the dreams for Marion's expansion. Population growth stalled, jobs were lost and fortunes evaporated. By 1933, movie attendance had fallen nationwide by 40 percent. In Marion, it was likely a larger decline. Those who could afford tickets bought them to escape. To counteract the possibility of an even larger decline, the Palace, like other theatres, reduced ticket prices, gave away dishes and offered sweepstakes. It even made an attempt to bring back vaudeville. Those who could not afford tickets needed escape the most. Ketchup soup—literally hot water and ketchup—got some through the day. As desperation increased, so did crime, and the Palace was robbed twice.

World War II brought the country, including Marion, out of the Great Depression. As money began to be more plentiful, entertainment

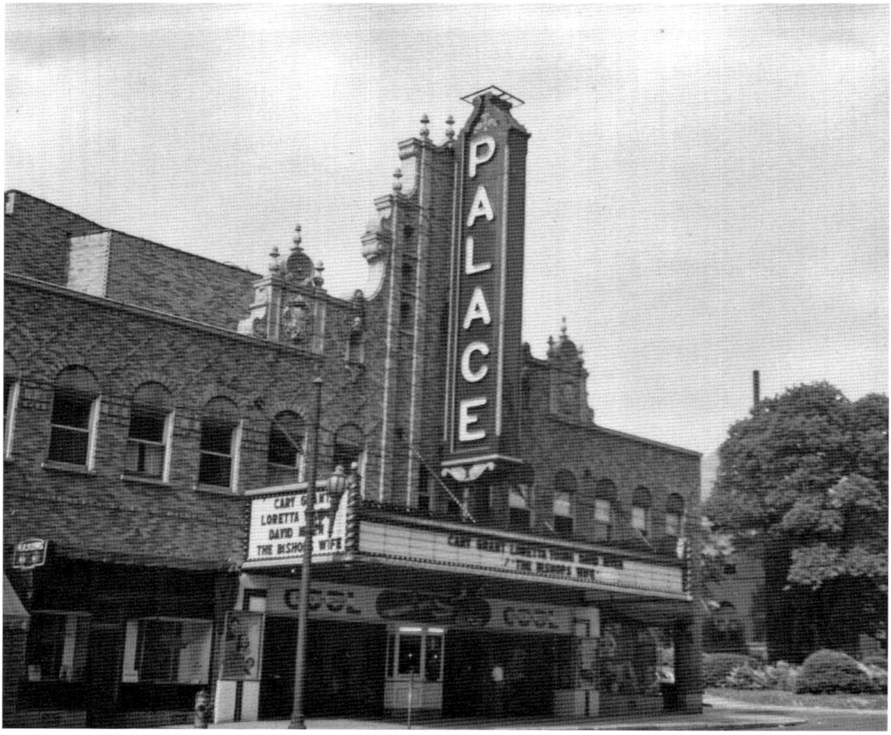

In 1947, the Palace air-conditioning system stopped working. When it was repaired, the front façade was covered with banners inviting patrons back to "relax in cool comfort." *Courtesy of the Marion County Historical Society.*

spending increased. Theatre attendance soared, and the Palace enjoyed a period of success. The Palace remained a destination for Marionites. It was part of their everyday life and was even authorized to sell war savings bonds at the ticket window.[1] While other, smaller theatres competed for the Palace's audience, the attraction of the atmospheric design kept the Palace seats full.

And then, as if someone had pushed a button, it ended again. This time, it was television. America fell in love with a new form of entertainment, and movie attendance again slumped. By the 1960s, television had replaced movie theatres as America's favorite pastime. In a March 30, 1963 article, "It's Real Murder at the Box Office," the *Marion Star* concluded that the Palace Theatre and the Ohio Theatre could not continue to stay in business.

The Palace, with a lease that would expire in July 1964, had to double attendance to 2,200 patrons a week. "My booker says, according to the amount of business the theatre is doing, Marion shows no indication of even wanting a theater," remarked Frank Dillon, manager of the Palace. Even *To Kill a Mockingbird*, nominated for eight Academy Awards, could not attract patrons. The *Star* reported that the movie averaged 180 a night during a seven-day run. The Palace averaged between 1,500 and 1,800 patrons a week in 1963. It then required 4,000 in paid attendance a week just to break even.

Even attendance by children, once a mainstay, had evaporated. Before 1959, 1,000 children regularly attended the movies on Saturdays. By 1963, that number had dropped to 200. But some events continued to draw patrons. The Palace sold 7,000 tickets in one week for the Disney movie *Flubber*. In February 1963, Junior Service Guild's presentation of *Cinderella* at the Palace sold 2,500 tickets for two shows.

By the start of the 1970s, average movie attendance at the Palace had fallen to fewer than fifty a performance. Movie theatres at shopping malls

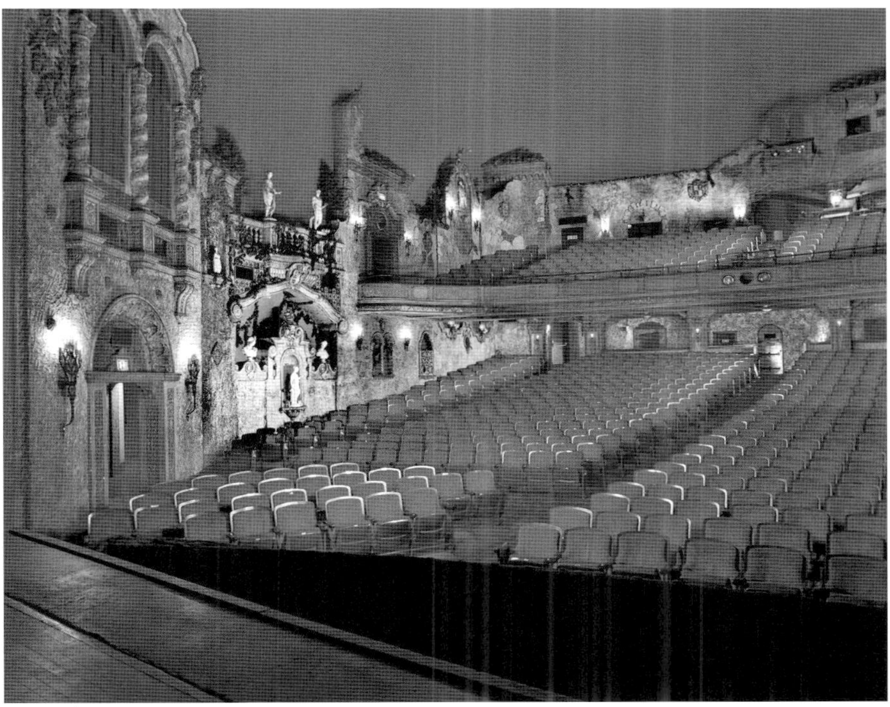

The interior of the Marion Palace Theatre today. This photograph, taken from the stage, shows a different perspective of the theatre's interior design. Many of the Caproni plaster reproduction statues that are placed along the east wall can be seen in this photograph. *Courtesy of Lew Lause. ©Lew Lause.*

took the bulk of the remaining moviegoers. There was no way out financially for a forty-five-year-old, energy-gobbling theatre. The Young Amusement Company sold the Palace on March 27, 1974, to Oren William Hatch. The price paid for the real estate was $60,000.[2]

Soon after, Hatch made the decision that the Palace would have to close. He considered an offer to demolish the building so that a service station could be built there and another to convert the building into a warehouse. On July 24, 1975, he sold the real estate to the Palace Cultural Arts Association for $78,000.[3] The nonprofit corporation was headed by Robert Babich, Lyle DeVilling, Frank Henson, John Keggan, George Lane, Ted Myers and Stephen Stuart, a group of community supporters who called themselves the Palace Guard. Their purpose was to restore the Palace and to operate it for the community. Less than a year later, $500,000 in donations had been raised. John Eberson's son, Drew, helped guide the restoration. The Palace reopened on July 8, 1976, with the musical *1776*.

Today, the Palace is operated as a nonprofit corporation, with a professional paid staff and hundreds of volunteers. Touring artists and community theatre productions keep it an active entertainment venue for Marion and the surrounding area. Recently, the May Pavilion, a 15,300-square-foot reception and event venue, was constructed beside the theatre. The Palace Theatre is listed on the National Register of Historic Places and is one of only sixteen Eberson atmospheric theatres still in operation.

PART I

ANOTHER THEATRE, ANOTHER TOWN

1

OVERTURE

A New Theatre Is Planned

At the end of the 1920s, the motion picture and theatre industries were booming. *Motion Picture News*, a combination business journal and gossip sheet, was widely read in the industry. In a small column in the January 7, 1928 issue, well beyond the front-page news, it was announced that Marion, Ohio, would have a new theatre:

> *John Eberson, prominent Chicago theatre architect, has been selected to develop the plans for the new Palace Theatre, to be built at Marion, Ohio, by the Young Amusement Co., V.U. Young, president, Gary, Indiana, in which project Ed. E. Bender and Sol Bernstein, Canton, Ohio, are also interested. The building is to house five stores and seven apartments in addition to the theatre.*[4]

For many of the readers, it was just another theatre in another town.

Everyone who glanced at the announcement knew about Marion, of course. President Warren G. Harding had conducted his front porch presidential campaign from Marion and received, along with Marion, widespread newsreel coverage. Even so, anyone who bothered to consider the news with more than a glance must have wondered whether Young would succeed in his plan to put large, lavish theatres in small Midwest towns, even if they had famous citizens.

The short article had very little information, other than the name, owner and location of the theatre. A few *Motion Picture News* readers would have known that the company's president, V.U. Young, was putting together a small string of motion picture and vaudeville theatres in Indiana and Ohio but had limited liquid capital. Much of what he owned was already invested in expensive theatre buildings.

Like many theatre developers, Young had to assemble capital for each new theatre. His associate, C.J. Wolf, of Wheeling, West Virginia, would be connected to the Marion investment, as he was for Young Amusement's Canton and Gary theatres. More funding was needed, and it would need to come from Ohio contacts, who knew Marion and who knew Young. The article made mention of that local funding, as if anticipating questions about the company's finances. Some of the capital would come from Edward E. Bender (owner of Bender's Restaurant, which still exists in Canton as of 2014) and Sol Bernstein, also of Canton. Both men had likely been impressed with the company's Palace Theatre in Canton, which opened in 1926. Additional funds would have to be generated by the building itself, with rent earned from stores and residential apartments.

Investments from Marion residents were not mentioned in this or later news reports. The *Marion Star* reported in July 1927 that no local capital would be used.[5] If local money was needed, Young certainly knew the right people necessary for introductions. Well-connected local residents David W. Evans and R.T. Lewis were largely responsible for the decision to locate a Young theatre in Marion.[6] But memories were long about another theatre built with local capital—the first Grand Opera House—and that theatre was not a financial success for investors.

The Marion Palace would be the company's third Eberson-designed theatre to be called by that name. It would join the Canton, Ohio Palace (1926) and the Gary, Indiana Palace (1925). All three Eberson atmospheric theatres would be referred to as Young's Wonder Theatres and as Young's million-dollar theatres. The Marion Palace investment was actually half that price, but its design was just as awe-inspiring to patrons.

Young and Wolf, like other theatre promoters, were constantly looking for new sites. The company's parameters were both geographic and economic. The site needed to be in Ohio or Indiana, near its other theatres. Also, the local community had to have a viable economy that would ensure financial success. Marion provided both. Geographically, Marion was near the company's Canton theatre. Located fifty miles north of Columbus, Marion was far enough away from the capital city's theatres to avoid direct competition with the better-funded theatre owners. Economically, Marion had the population needed to support the scaled-down atmospheric theatre, and its strong industrial base convinced the company that it was a good growth opportunity.[7] A new, grand, eight-story hotel, completed in 1924, stood across the street. If the town could support a hotel of that size and quality, Young and Wolf reasoned that it could also support a new theatre.[8]

Acquisition of the site for the theatre was announced in Marion on July 19, 1927.[9] It was a preliminary announcement since almost nothing had been determined other than that John Eberson would design an atmospheric theatre in a Spanish style that would seat between 1,500 and 2,000 patrons.[10] The company also announced that the theatre would be designed for motion pictures, vaudeville and "legitimate" theatre (meaning plays rather than vaudeville or musicals).[11] Immediately after the announcement was made, Young left Marion for Chicago, where he met with Eberson and his architects to start the design plans.[12]

On December 23, 1927, Marion saw the Palace for the first time. Eberson's drawing of the theatre was printed on the front page of the *Marion Star*, with the news that the architecture would indeed be Spanish and that the construction contract had been signed.[13] Construction work was to begin immediately after Christmas, with the opening scheduled for Labor Day 1928.[14] Once again, Evans and Lewis were involved as they presided over the announcement to the press and were on hand to answer questions.[15]

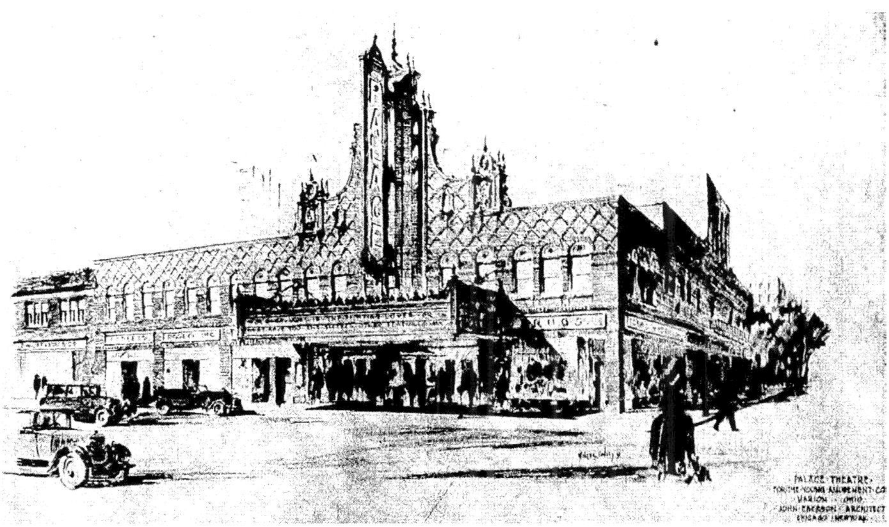

An architectural sketch of the Palace Theatre appeared in the *Marion Daily Star* on December 23, 1927, the first glimpse Marion had of the Palace. *Courtesy of the* Marion Daily Star.

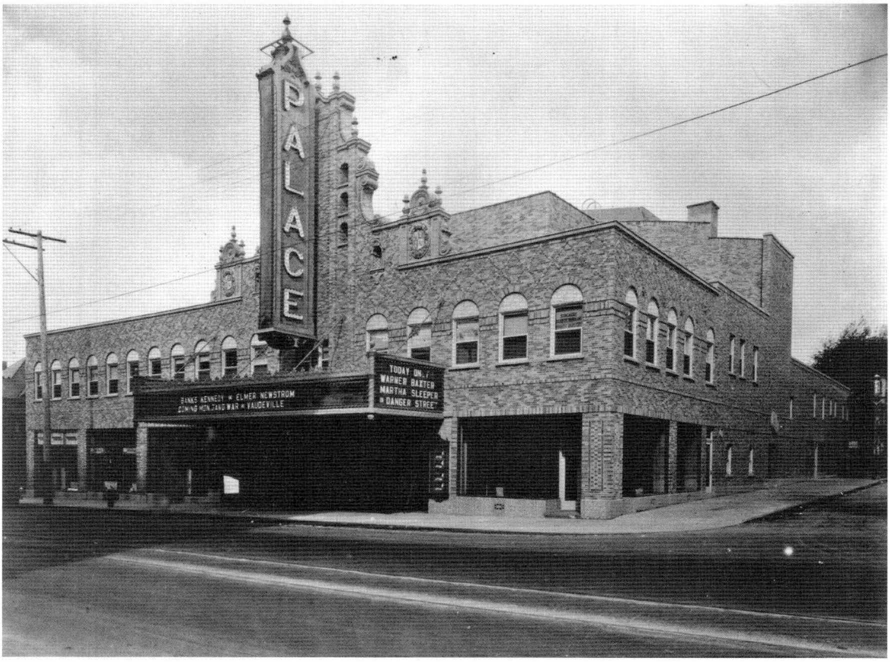

The Marion Palace Theatre as it looked on Sunday, September 22, 1928. The polychrome technique of brick placement creates exterior patterns that highlight the building's architectural features. *Courtesy of the Marion County Historical Society.*

The theatre would have a large stage for vaudeville and legitimate theatre, which would accommodate even the largest productions.[16] The latest movie projection equipment, lighting and mechanical devices were to be installed.[17] A concert symphony orchestra could be accommodated in the orchestra pit, and a large organ would rise out of the pit to provide music and effects for silent motion pictures.[18] It would be like nothing else in Marion—or almost all of Ohio, for that matter.

The actors were not forgotten in the plans. Large, well-ventilated dressing rooms would be provided, some with baths and showers. To attract top talent, well-equipped dressing rooms were essential.[19]

The building would be constructed of steel, concrete, brick and stone. On the front façade, brick and stone would be used, with finishes of terra cotta (a clay-based ceramic) and polychrome (different colored bricks used to create a design or highlight architectural elements). At the Palace, polychrome would be used to create a crisscross pattern, and terra cotta would be used for exterior ornamentation.[20]

The 1927 plans included seating for two thousand patrons.[21] This was later revised downward because the site was not large enough for that number of seats. A three-story lobby, which the contractor boasted would be one of the most beautiful in Ohio, was later eliminated. Such changes would not have been unusual, as the owner, contractor and architect came to terms with the finite amount of money available to construct and decorate the building and any building constraints caused by the shape or size of the building lot. No original plans survive, so the reasons for the modifications to the original plans are unknown.

Few in Marion had seen an atmospheric theatre, and most had no idea what was being described. In eight months, they would see it for themselves.

PART II

A THEATRE TO OPEN

2

OPENING NIGHT

August 30, 1928

V.U. Young arrived back in Marion on Tuesday, August 21, 1928.[22] In a trip he had made many times over the last year by train and automobile, Young came this time not to plan but to open his newest theatre: the Marion Palace. His co-owner, C.J. Wolf, was in Marion as well. Wolf lived in Wheeling, West Virginia, and was president of the Young Amusement Company.[23] Less than a year before, the architect and contractor had promised that the Palace would be open before Labor Day.[24] Although the company had not announced a date to Marion, the theatre would open even before then.

The Palace would become the company's tenth theatre.[25] The company had started operations in 1910 with its first theatre, the Orpheum in Gary, Indiana, where Young lived.[26] Eighteen years later, the company had expanded to own a chain of theatres that stretched from Chicago to the Cleveland suburbs, including Gary and Kokomo in Indiana and Canton, Ohio. Another theatre was under construction in Anderson, Indiana. It was a lot of geography to cover, but there was a lot of money to be made.

Young actually preferred to fly to his theatres using his own airplane. It was a Velie Monocoupe, a wooden-framed, fabric-covered sport plane that seated two people in the enclosed cabin.[27] It could reach speeds of up to 150 miles per hour.[28] With his brother Martin piloting, Young could visit two of the company's theatres in a day.[29]

He had flown to Marion only once, on June 21, 1928.[30] Once was enough. Marion had no landing field, and Young's plane had to land using a small field on the McNeal farm, west of the city.[31] It was a landing spot suggested by local realtor R.T. Lewis, who had sent Young a map and landmark information.[32] Landing on fields was risky. Until Marion developed a modern airfield, Young decided to stay on the ground.[33]

By the time the Palace opened, Marion had made modest progress in developing an airport. That decision was reached by the Marion City Council on August 13, 1928,[34] and the first commercial flight, which carried radio parts, landed on the new airfield on August 24.[35] Young now felt that it was safe for his plane to land in Marion and had his brother fly it there on the Saturday before the opening.[36] But he was about to learn that Marion was not quite ready for the aviation age.

After landing at Marion's new airport, Martin left for the city, but not before looking back to make sure everything was in order.[37] When he returned later that day, he discovered that the plane had been damaged by a mule. The animal had roamed away from a nearby pasture and eaten fabric from the wing and stabilizer. The plane was grounded, and it cost Young $180 (about $2,500 in 2014 dollars) to fix it.[38] It was repaired on Sunday and Monday, and Martin wasted no time the next morning taking off for Gary.[39] Left behind to open his tenth theatre, Young hoped the people of Marion would be kinder to him—and his money—than the mule.

Even before Young reached the Harding Hotel, where he would stay for the week and the opening, he saw the sign. John Eberson insisted on two signs for his theatres: a horizontal marquee to advertise the shows and a huge vertical sign that could be seen from blocks away to announce the theatre's name. Many theatre owners could afford only a marquee, but Eberson's additional sign was well worth the cost. Young wanted everyone to remember that the theatre was open, no matter where they were standing on Center Street.

The vertical blade sign was sixty feet above street level.[40] Each of the letters—P-A-L-A-C-E—was six feet high and outlined with flashing lights.[41] Marion had never had a sign like this before. It could be seen from a mile away.[42]

For those who didn't work or shop downtown, about fifteen large publicity signs, measuring twelve by twenty feet, were constructed around Marion County and its surrounding areas.[43] Each announced the opening of the Palace as Marion's only atmospheric theatre.[44]

By the time Young had arrived in Marion to prepare for the opening, most of the employees were already there. Albert E. Sindlinger was hired as the general manager.[45] Young had asked him to arrive in Marion from his Athens home on the same day as Young and Wolf so they could

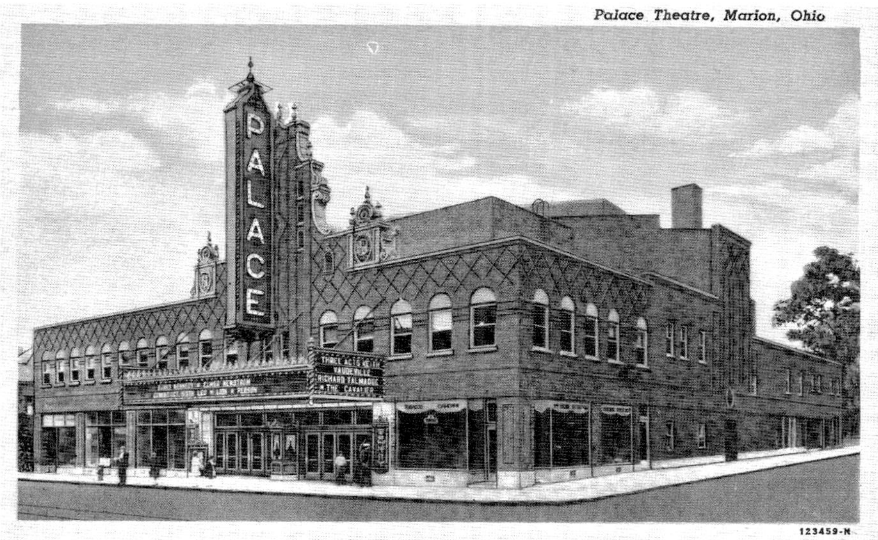

A September 28, 1928 postcard view of the Marion Palace. The marquee advertises the silent film *Cavalier* and three acts of vaudeville. It announced that MGM's *Leo the Lion* would be coming soon to make a live appearance. *Author's collection.*

coordinate the final details. A fifteen-year theatre veteran, Sindlinger knew his job inside and out. He had worked at theatres since he was thirteen, as manager, electrician, cameraman, stagehand and once even as an actor on the Chautauqua stage.[46] His experience as an electrician would be helpful in the atmospheric theatre and would be particularly important when the equipment for the "talkies" arrived in the spring.

W.E. Bail was assistant manager and publicity director.[47] A young man, Bail had been with Young Amusement Company for four years, most recently in Canton as manager of the Lyceum Theatre and as publicity director for three other theatres.[48] Before working in theatres, Bail had been a reporter for the *Post Tribune* (Gary, Indiana), and he knew how to work local reporters for good coverage.[49] Bail had given the *Star* reporters enough information for an entire supplement to the paper, which he was assured would run the day before the opening.

The last vacancies to fill were the ushers, scheduled to be interviewed and hired on August 25.[50] In most theatres, no one walked down the aisle without an usher, and there was an average of two ushers per aisle per shift.[51] That staffing formula would require at least sixteen ushers (four orchestra aisles and four balcony aisles) and a head usher. For older boys and young men, ushering at the Palace was a desirable job. The uniforms were handsome and commanded respect. Free passes for friends and relatives made them very popular.

The Palace also required a stage manager, at least two stagehands, a projectionist, an assistant projectionist, two box office staff members, a custodian and a building supervisor. At a minimum, the payroll would include twenty-eight people on the operations side of the house and backstage. On the artistic side, employees would include the orchestra director, the musicians and the organist.

Timing a new theatre's opening date was tricky business. When dark, a theatre produced no revenue, so it was essential to open it as soon as possible. Yet that required booking acts and motion pictures, hiring employees, coordinating the organist and orchestra performances, sending VIP invitations and all manner of other details far in advance. Any problem with the contractor or a supplier could throw everything into chaos. The owners had learned to simply set a date and make the people hit it. For Marion, that date was Thursday, August 30, 1928.

More than anything, both Young and Wolf wanted to open the Palace with the newest sound picture technology. The company had ordered both the Movietone and the Vitaphone systems, but neither would be available on opening night.[52] No amount of prodding helped.

Movietone was a new technology that recorded the sound on the film itself and was used primarily for newsreels. Vitaphone, also new, used a separate recorded disc for sound playback and was employed for moving pictures. Young and Wolf knew that motion pictures and newsreels with sound were absolutely essential to the theatre's success. However, the manufacturers could not satisfy the demand. Too many theatres wanted the same thing at the same time, and their ten-theatre company had minimal buying power. They—and Marion—would need to wait until the spring of the following year for the equipment to be installed.[53]

To prepare for sound, the company had the projection room and auditorium pre-wired for the new equipment. In fact, the entire theatre was designed for sound motion pictures, using the manufacturers' specifications for the best sound reproduction and amplification.[54] Young told the *Star* that he had "solid faith" in sound and talking pictures and wanted to give Marion the latest and best technology possible.[55]

The company also needed Marion to pay for the sound and every other part of the half-million-dollar Palace. At the tail end of the Roaring Twenties, many Americans—those still in the lower economic classes—had a bit more leisure time and money in their pockets. They were attending theatres in

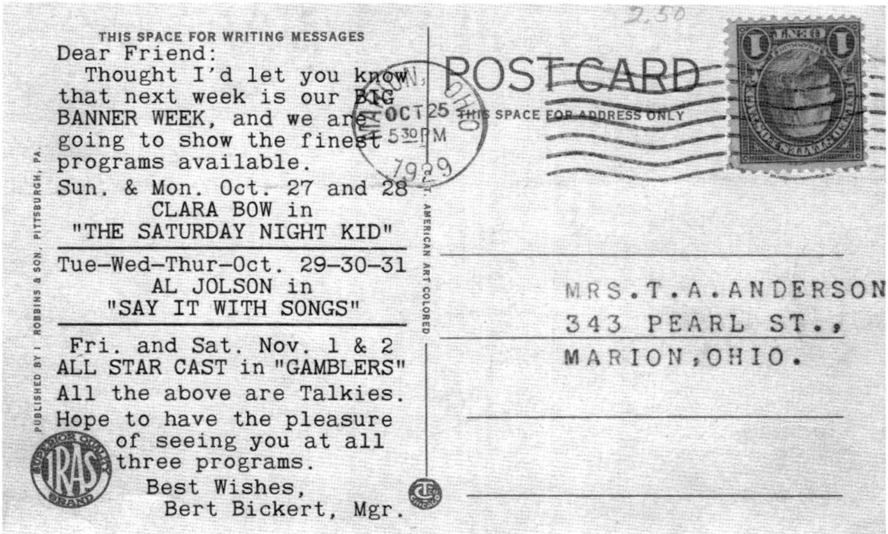

THIS SPACE FOR WRITING MESSAGES

Dear Friend:
Thought I'd let you know that next week is our BIG BANNER WEEK, and we are going to show the finest programs available.

Sun. & Mon. Oct. 27 and 28
CLARA BOW in
"THE SATURDAY NIGHT KID"

Tue-Wed-Thur-Oct. 29-30-31
AL JOLSON in
"SAY IT WITH SONGS"

Fri. and Sat. Nov. 1 & 2
ALL STAR CAST in "GAMBLERS"

All the above are Talkies.
Hope to have the pleasure of seeing you at all three programs.

Best Wishes,
Bert Bickert, Mgr.

POST CARD

THIS SPACE FOR ADDRESS ONLY

OCT 25 5:30 PM 1929

MRS.T.A.ANDERSON
343 PEARL ST.,
MARION,OHIO.

PUBLISHED BY I. ROBBINS & SON, PITTSBURGH, PA.

AMERICAN ART COLORED

Above: Postcards were used to advertise upcoming shows. This card was postmarked on Black Tuesday. The coming Great Depression would close the Palace for seven weeks. *Courtesy of the Mike and Linda Perry Collection.*

Right: Volume 1, issue 1 of the first Palace newsletter, dated September 23, 1928. The newsletter was published weekly and included the program for the week ahead. *Courtesy of the Palace Cultural Arts Association.*

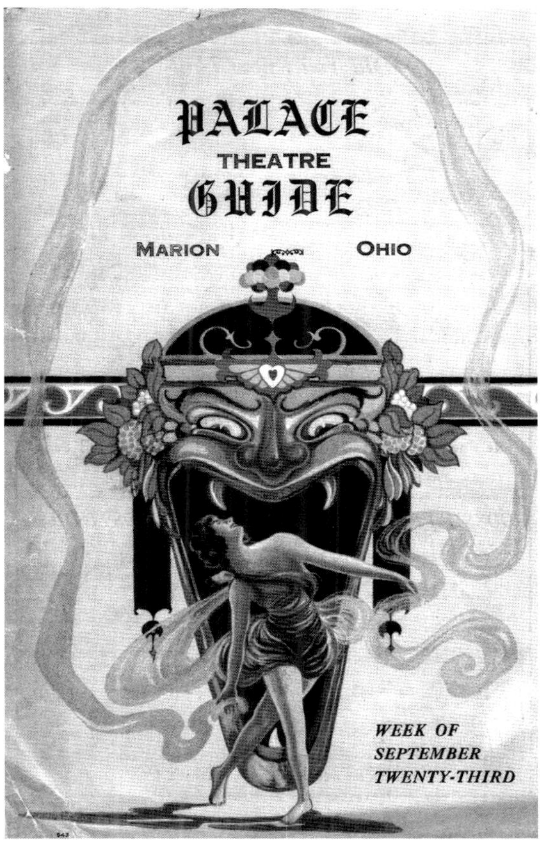

droves. But it was not cheap. The average ticket price of $0.25 to $0.50 was equal to $3.30 to $6.50 in 2014 dollars.

Eberson had clearly delivered what he had promised Young: a Spanish garden on a hill. When Young entered the theatre, he didn't see the clouds that would be produced by the Brenkert Brenograph Jr. projector—they would be ready opening night—but he did see a courtyard garden in the middle of a palace on a hill in Mediterranean Spain. It could have been in Seville or Grenada.

The Marion Palace closely resembled the Spanish Revival architecture that was then very popular in Florida—arches, terra-cotta roof tiles, towerlike structures, balconies, ornamental ironwork, courtyards, patios and arcades. Young did not want the minarets or keyhole arches that were representative of a Moorish design.[56] Instead, the design influence of the Spanish architect José Benito de Churriguera was prevalent. This Churrigueresque style could be seen in the pillars to the right of the stage, the proscenium details and throughout the interior design. It appeared also in Eberson's use of balustrades, stucco shells and garlands.

It was impossible to assign a precise style to any of Eberson's theatres, Young knew. That was not the point. He mixed architectural styles, more interested in evoking an impression than precisely replicating an architectural period. Young saw that done throughout the Marion Palace, including the placement of Greek bas-relief urns that separate the mezzanine (middle stairway) and balcony levels on the staircase. The urns have nothing at all to do with Spain, but they did *suggest* the riches of a palace.

The day before the opening, the *Star* took readers inside the Palace with a detailed story. The headline read, "Interior of House Perfect in Details—Spanish Design and Atmospheric Effect Make Scene of Rare Beauty—Art Masterpiece—Decorations, Architecture and Furnishings Blend to Form Entrancing Picture."[57]

> *Forget for a few minutes that you are reading a copy of your evening paper. Allow your imagination to carry you to the gentle slope of a moon-lit Spanish hill.*
>
> *Before you rise* [sic] *a vine covered garden wall, broken here and there with graceful arches. Through the archways spreads the soft light of a harvest moon and the dim glow casts shadows over the somber colored walls.*
>
> *Overhead myriads of stars are twinkling in an azure blue sky and soft, fleecy clouds are drifting gently with the breeze.*
>
> *Picture all this in your mind and you have a fair conception of the interior of the Palace theater—Marion's new half million dollar playhouse.*

The new theater is Spanish in design in all its details. From the walls and the mural decorations to the reproduction of period furniture in the lounges the Spanish design is followed.

Before going to the Palace for the first time Thursday night it might be well to take a word tour through the new playhouse.

The boxoffice is approached directly from the street. Inside double swinging doors is the lobby. After passing through more double doors one enters the foyer and the theater proper.

The doors separating the foyer and the lobby are made of heavy walnut and are in keeping with the interior decorations. Deep grooves line their surface, giving them a weather-beaten appearance. Small openings near the top are barred with iron gratings.

Four aisles lead from the foyer to the orchestra seats, two from the ends of the foyer and two between. The foyer floor as well as the aisles is covered with a heavy carpet. To aid patrons in finding their places each end seat is fitted with a light which illuminates the floor. The seats are upholstered in red leather and are made comfortable with thick padding and springs. The backs of seats are also leather upholstered.

Opportunities for carrying out the Spanish effect in the mezzanine floor are even greater than in the foyer. Here the designer of the theater has let his fancy take full flight. Here and there patches of red brick appear, as through [sic] *the plaster had fallen from the walls. A niche in the wall is cleverly adapted to hold a drinking fountain.*

The view from the balcony is even better than the lower floor. As in the lower floor view of the stage is unobstructed by pillars. [The] *balcony being of cantilever construction removes the necessity of supporting it with posts and pillars which necessarily cut off the view of the unfortunate patron who is forced to sit behind one.*

From the balcony one obtains a broad sweeping view of the entire theater. Although there is nothing to hamper visibility from the lower floor one obtains a better prospectus of the theater from the balcony. There is no second balcony in the Palace.

Emergency exits from the theater with the exception of one fire escape on the west side are all built within the walls of the building.

With the exception of the commercial section in front of the building including office rooms on the second floor and business rooms on the ground floor, the structure is strictly fire-proof.[58]

Bail, the Palace's publicity director, had done his job well.

Weather reports for the opening were favorable. A heat wave had kept the temperatures in the nineties all week. It broke on opening day. Highs were expected to be only in the low eighties, with nighttime temperatures falling to fifty-five degrees. No rain was predicted. It could not have been better weather.

A rehearsal of the opening was held the morning of August 30, 1928.[59] Manager Albert Sindlinger was in charge. The orchestra, directed by Elmer Newstrom, played its numbers. The Page organ was tested by Banks Kennedy. The first reel of the motion picture looped through the projection machine. The stagehands set the lights for the cues and made everything else backstage ready to function. As the various Keith-Albee vaudeville circuit acts arrived, Newstrom and the orchestra practiced cues as the actors rehearsed. The ushers were inspected and received last-minute instructions on how to quickly and safely seat 1,540 people.[60] It seemed that the building itself was holding its breath.

Young expected 3,200 people for the two opening night performances.[61] The first was scheduled to start at 6:30 p.m. and the second at 9:15 p.m. Admission for the first performance was twenty-five cents and for the second, fifty cents. A child's ticket cost ten cents.

A small number of invitations were sent to people who were connected with the construction of the theatre.[62] They entered the Campbell Street doors between 6:00 and 6:30 p.m.[63] It was a generous gift to those who built the theatre.

At 6:30 p.m., the lobby doors were opened to paying patrons.[64] Delays in seating were caused by patrons who walked into the theatre and stopped in the aisles, unable to move their gaze from the twinkling stars and billowing clouds above or the Spanish architecture around them.[65] The *Marion Star* reported that the eyes of the awestricken guests moved in eight different directions at once.[66]

They would have many opportunities to come again. The original schedule in 1928 was to show movies and vaudeville on Thursday, Friday and Saturday and movies only from Sunday to Wednesday.

Unlike other theatre openings, the speeches were kept to a minimum. Colonel George B. Christian gave a brief opening address.[67] He spoke at only the first performance. The father of President Harding's secretary, George B. Christian Jr., he was actively involved in Marion's civic life. His remarks included a short history of theatres in Marion, and he praised the beauty of the building.[68]

Eberson then made a few remarks and introduced Young.[69] He presented Young with a bag of birdseed, a tongue-in-cheek reference to the stuffed

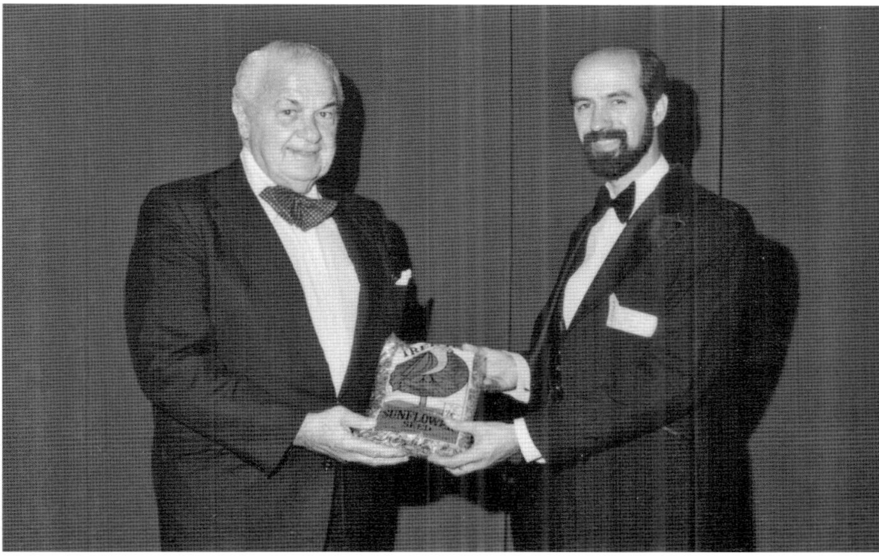

John Eberson's son, Drew, presented a bag of birdseed to the Palace Cultural Arts Association at the fiftieth-anniversary celebration of the theatre's opening night. *Courtesy of the Palace Cultural Arts Association.*

pigeons that Eberson had installed to create the feeling of being outdoors at the Palace.[70] He made the same gift to theatre owners at every opening.[71]

He also joked with Young about the damage a mule had done to Mr. Young's airplane at the local airport. Eberson, a Democrat, told Young, an ardent Republican, that the mule must have been a Democrat.[72]

The entertainment began with organ music by Banks Kennedy, a well-known Chicago organist who had previously performed at the Canton Palace Theatre.[73] The largest applause of the evening came when the organ was raised to stage level, played by Kennedy.[74] He had written a new composition, which he titled "Everybody's Welcome to the Palace." Next was a theatre overture, "A Night in the Clock Store," by the Palace Orchestra under the direction of Elmer Newstrom.[75]

The Keith-Albee vaudeville acts followed. Harry Kahne, a nationally known mental wizard, was the first act. He kept audiences enthralled by such mental feats as reciting a poem while upside down and simultaneously writing three long words backward and upside down. Tilyou and Rogers, a comedy team, were featured in a short routine, "A Younger Generation," about youth and old age. In the act, they impersonated an old man doing slow-motion tumbles. Johnny Mack and Company (including

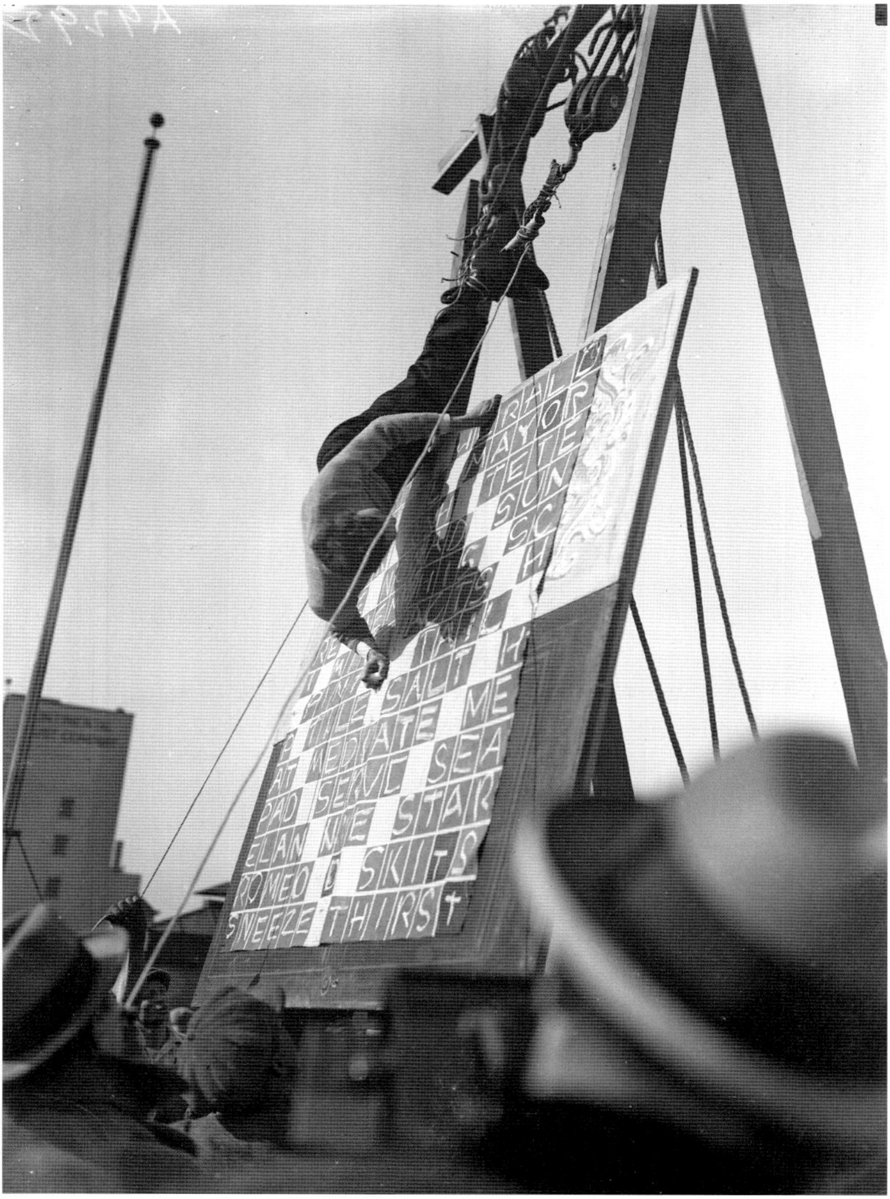

Vaudeville star Harry Kahne (1895–1955), the original multitasker, was able to concentrate on several mental activities at the same time. He appeared on opening night at the Marion Palace. *Courtesy of the Library of Congress.*

Ethel Dunton, Dolly Moran and Shirley Manion) performed in "Dance Bits." They entertained the opening night patrons with both serious and comedic dance routines.

The Palace management had received advance notice that Harry Kahne might not make the opening, so the theatre added a fourth act, the Castlemans, a trio of entertainers. They had just completed appearances at several theatres on the Orpheum Circuit and were on their way to Chicago.

Next was the Metro-Goldwin-Mayer silent picture *Excess Baggage* starring William Haines, Josephine Dunn and Ricardo Cortez. It was a behind-the-scenes movie about the small-time vaudeville circuit and the performers whose greatest ambition was to make it big in New York City. The movie was based on the stage play of the same name, which was still playing in Chicago.

At 10:10 p.m., West Center and Campbell Streets were filled with over three thousand people.[76] The first of two opening night performances had ended, and patrons were leaving the theatre via the Campbell Street exit doors. The lobby was completely full of people holding tickets for the second performance, which was almost an hour late in starting. The line to buy tickets extended up Center Street, three and four deep, past the entrance to Central Junior High School located east of the Palace.

At 1:00 a.m., the second show ended, and the patrons left. The Palace had opened and had earned its first money: about $1,000 in opening night receipts.

The day after the opening, the *Marion Star* editorial, titled "A Splendid New Theater," expressed excitement that the Palace had exceeded all expectations:

> *Experience has taught the most of us that very often performance lacks something of promise. As a rule, the lions on the billboards are larger, fiercer and far more impressive than those in view under the tent when show day comes.*
>
> *So much has been said by those who had had opportunity to view the new Palace theater, the beauty of its commodious interior had been so lauded by them, that we feared the possibility that the general rule might prove to hold in connection with it; that over expectations carried to high pitch might fall short of realization.*
>
> *The thousands who attended its opening last night found the Palace the exception to the rule—a marked exception in that its beauty, the artistry and its comfort combined to make it a place of amusement far and away*

> *beyond anything that reports concerning it could possibly have established in the public mind.*
>
> *There are many splendid theaters in the state of Ohio, many which are places of delight, but it is to be questioned if any of them has a charm exceeding that of the new theater on west Center street.*
>
> *It is often said of such enterprises that they are worthy of the cities they grace. It may be said in the present case that Marion will have to be up and doing to be worthy of the new place of amusement which the Young Amusement company opened to the public last night.*[77]

Just as Young and Wolf had hoped.

PART III

JOHN EBERSON AND HIS ATMOSPHERIC THEATRES

3

OPERA HOUSE JOHN

A Flair for the Dramatic

Frances Mather, a writer for *National* magazine, succinctly described Palace Theatre architect John Eberson in her popular Washington, D.C. "Mostly About People" column. She wrote that Eberson was

> *a man of great conceptions, carried out to the tiniest practical detail. He is more than an architect, however, for in executing his revolutionary innovations in theater building, he follows in the footsteps of the great Michelangelo. Employing many arts, Mr. Eberson is at once architect, engineer, interior decorator and mural painter, using artificial lighting as well as brushes to gain his color effect and he applies all this knowledge in creating his contribution to the modern theatre—the outdoor illusion.*[78]

Few architects enjoyed this level of media attention.

With his atmospheric theatres, Eberson had responded to the mood of America. The country was defining itself by a new breed of Michelangelos of commerce. It was ready for American commercialism, legitimated in design by Old World respectability. Eberson developed an illusion of wealth, where the working and middle classes could believe that they *had* achieved a better, richer and fuller life.

That they had not achieved wealth was what Eberson tried to hide and what America wanted hidden. Despite the popular image today, the 1920s was far from a decade of prosperity. Two-thirds of American families lived—in desperation—on incomes of less than $2,500, which was the official minimum

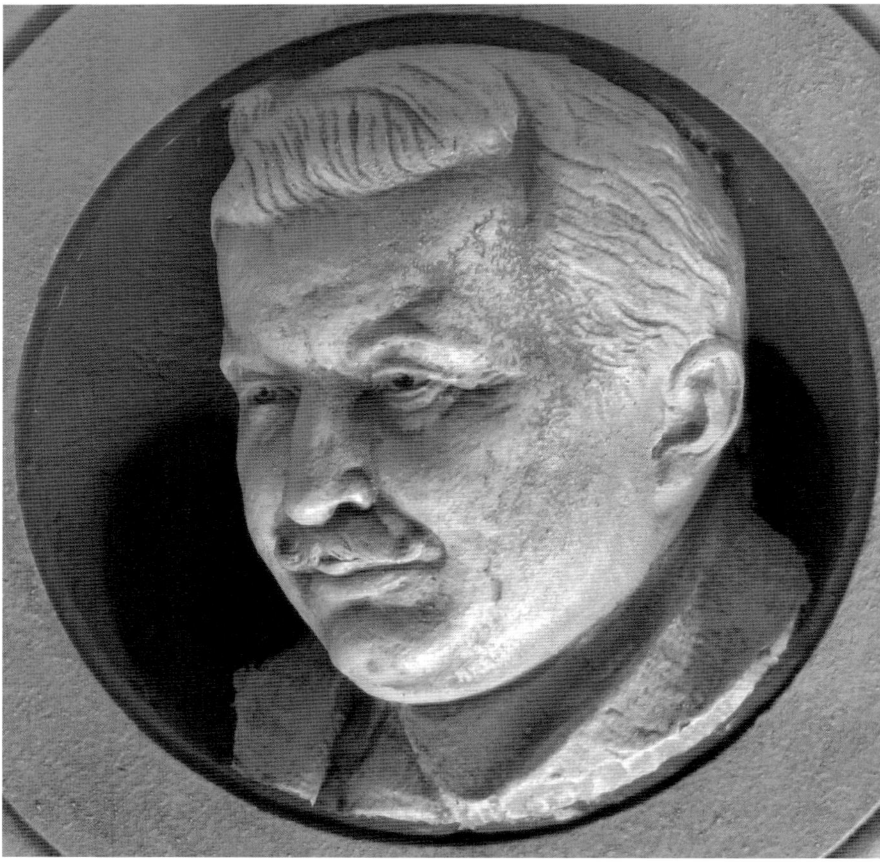

The bust of John Eberson that appears on the vaulted ceiling of the grand foyer in the Palace Theatre in Louisville, Kentucky. *Author's collection.*

for a "decent" living.[79] For most, the American dream was achieved only on the movie screen. In a very real way, Eberson's theatres echoed F. Scott Fitzgerald's last line in his 1925 novel *The Great Gatsby*: "So we beat on, boats against the current, borne back ceaselessly into the past."

He was born John Adolf Emil Eberson on January 2, 1875.[80] During his career, which did not end until his death in 1954, he was best known for his development and promotion of the atmospheric style of theatre. Designed to immerse the patron in an illusion of a lavish Old World outdoor setting, the atmospheric design was reproduced in many of his theatres. Over the decades, he and his firm designed a significant number of theatres, approximately one hundred of which were in the atmospheric design, almost all in the eastern two-thirds of the United States.[81] Sources differ on the exact count. Clients included small, regional companies (like the Young Amusement Company, which built the Marion Palace) and theatre giants (including Paramount, Loew's, Universal and Warner Brothers).[82]

Born in Cernauti, Bukovina, part of Austria-Hungary, John was the son of Sigfried and Lora (Schmidt) Eberson.[83] His father was a timber cruiser and shipper of white pine to America.[84] John was educated in Dresden, Saxony, and studied electrical engineering at the University of Vienna. As a young man, he led an active student life. Eberson's son, Drew, recalled, "He had engaged in several duels, as was the custom in the fraternities of the European universities, and bore scars in testimony to what was considered friendly competition."[85]

Soon after he completed his studies in 1896, Eberson joined the Fourteenth Hussaren Regiment of the Austrian army, a light cavalry unit, a privilege extended only to college graduates.[86] Within the first year, he was jailed after an altercation with a regiment officer and formally imprisoned.[87] He eventually immigrated to America in 1901.[88]

He boarded a ship to America in Bremerhaven Harbor, with little more than a passport and one hundred florins.[89] Upon arrival in New York, he did what many immigrants did in the early 1900s: he settled in an area where he would be welcomed in a strange land. For Eberson, this was in St. Louis, an area with an established Austrian and German community.[90] He learned English in St. Louis by studying at home and by listening to sermons at church and soon developed an excellent command of the language.[91]

His first job in St. Louis was with an electrical contracting company in which he put to use his electrical studies in Vienna.[92] Although sources on Eberson's life differ, he may have actually started and owned the business.[93]

After two years, Eberson began an informal relationship with Johnson Realty and Construction Company, a theatre architectural, construction and promotion company headed by George J. Johnson.[94] Eberson met Johnson while installing electrical components in a Vicksburg, Mississippi theatre.[95] The company had expertise in scenic design and theatre promotion and construction.[96] It is believed that he was never an employee of the company, but he did head the architectural department.[97]

Johnson traveled around the country convincing small towns to build opera houses. Once convinced that an opera house was perfect for their town, citizens hired Eberson to prepare the plans and specifications and Johnson to build it.[98] One author joked that this arrangement sounded "a bit like the set-up for *The Music Man*, but Johnson was apparently not Prof.

Harold Hill and the collaboration proved quite successful, earning Eberson the nickname of 'Opera House John.'"[99] The relationship with Johnson lasted more than six years.

His early commissions were traditional theatre designs—large rectangular boxes with ornate ceilings.[100] The designs reflected the dual uses of a theatre building: exhibition of live theatre and silent motion pictures. They were long, rectangular spaces, with a stage at one end and room for an organ or piano.[101] An L-shaped design was typical, with an entry lobby at a right angle to the auditorium.[102] The film projectionist was at street level with the audience, allowing for a quick escape if the highly volatile nitrocellulose film caught on fire.[103]

In addition to what Eberson learned from his work with Johnson, other architectural ideas and inspiration surely came from the 1904 St. Louis World's Fair. While most of the twenty million visitors would have been intrigued by the ice cream cone and the X-ray machine, Eberson was likely most impressed by the extensive display of electricity. Some have speculated that the fair may have inspired his unique ideas about atmospheric theatre lighting, including the reproduction of a nighttime sky with twinkling lights on a theatre dome.[104]

Eberson was probably influenced by the use of cheap building materials to create architectural elements that decorated the many temporary buildings on the fairgrounds.[105] It was an inexpensive building technique that was first used by Daniel Burnham at the World's Columbian Exhibition in 1893 in Chicago.[106] The buildings were finished and decorated with a cheap building material that could be molded or shaped into various designs. Called *staff*, the material was a mixture of lime plaster and cement, which contained glycerin and dextrose. A bond was created in this mixture by the addition of Manila hemp fibers (the main ingredient in rope). It could be poured into molds, shaped with knives, hammered and sawed and was a perfect substance to create lavish, inexpensive architectural effects.

With that many people passing through St. Louis for the fair and Eberson's interest in theatre architecture, it was not surprising that he met people who would later have an influence on his life. It was as a result of the fair that Eberson met Karl Hoblitzelle of the Interstate Theater Company, who would later retain him to design theatres in Texas, including the then-unique Dallas Majestic Theatre, which opened in 1921.[107]

Eberson married Beatrice Lamb (1885–1954) in 1903. She was an immigrant from London and an interior decorator by trade. Later, this background resulted in Beatrice's becoming a significant contributor to the design of her husband's theatre interiors.[108]

In 1904, the Ebersons moved to Hamilton, Ohio, on the banks of the Great Miami River near Cincinnati.[109] When the Ebersons arrived, Hamilton was a bustling industrial town. Eberson continued his relationship with Johnson until 1908, when he opened his own architectural firm at 304 Rentschler Building in Hamilton. His first commissioned job was that same year, when he designed an Ionic-columned porch for Mrs. Sheehan, a Hamilton resident, for which he received twenty dollars.[110]

In Hamilton, he was commissioned for industrial and commercial buildings in the area. It was there that he designed and supervised construction of his first theatre, the Hamilton Jewel, just up the street from his architectural office. In a pre–Civil War building, he designed a 350-seat theatre in a forty-by fifty-foot space.[111] The building was razed in 1926.

Eberson and his family moved to Chicago in 1910 to pursue his theatrical architecture career, which he had nurtured since he left St. Louis.[112] Hamilton had been his home for six years, and it was not without some regret that he left. In a later letter to the Hamilton newspaper, Eberson's close connections with Hamilton were evident:

> *I certainly have a warm spot in my heart for Hamilton, and with recollections and experiences of my earlier life spent in Hamilton, never to be forgotten, with friendships established in Hamilton which I cherish very highly. I am sure that all of our old friends and neighbors in Hamilton will be glad to know that all of my family are enjoying the best of health. Mrs. Eberson is fine and a proud grandmother.*
>
> *My son Drew, a graduate of the University of Pennsylvania, has earned his spurs and is a licensed architect and full partner with me. Lora Mary, my oldest daughter, is married and has a very fine boy about a year old. My youngest daughter, Elsa, is attending an Eastern school, and as time goes, she is our baby and twenty years old.*
>
> *We are maintaining a large architectural organization in Chicago as well as New York and I spend my time commuting between those two burgs. We are particularly proud to have earned the confidence and clientele of so many large theatrical syndicates, which has opportuned us to sell our services not only in interstate fashion in the United States, but also in Europe and Australia.*[113]

Hamilton was proud of the Ebersons, and the feeling was mutual.

Once in Chicago, he enjoyed a steady flow of theatre architectural work. Karl Hoblitzelle's Interstate Amusement Company provided the

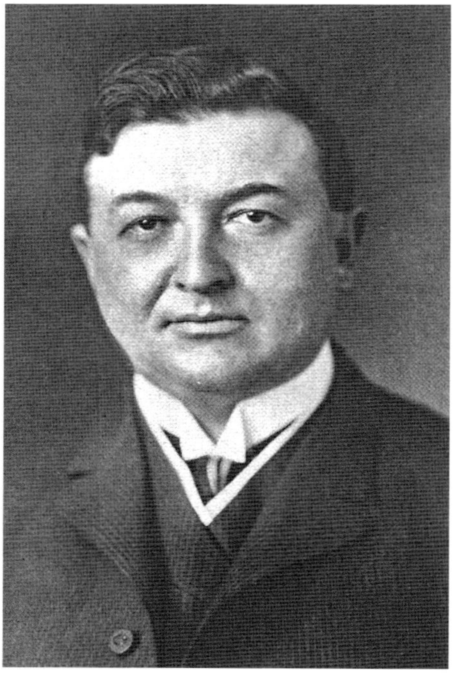

A portrait of John Eberson, around 1910, following his move from Hamilton, Ohio, to Chicago. *Author's collection.*

first major commissions.[114] These were the Majestic (Fort Worth, 1911) and the Majestic (Austin, 1915). However, neither design was groundbreaking.[115]

Eberson's greatest architectural success—the atmospheric design—began with two later theatres he created for Hoblitzelle: the Wichita Orpheum (1922) and the Dallas Majestic (1921). In 1922, with the design of the Houston Majestic, Eberson created his first full atmospheric design for Hoblitzelle. The Houston Majestic opened on January 29, 1923. It was as if Eberson had returned to his childhood. The landscapes, gardens, fountains, statuary and other design elements were all impressions of Europe.

For the first time, the theatre design became the event. Eberson firmly believed that to be a successful theatre architect, he had to be a showman.[116] The Majestic had intensely classical walls, with a reproduction of the Porch of the Maidens on the Acropolis. To create the atmosphere, he included a plain, undecorated ceiling, onto which were projected moving clouds. The show enveloped the theatre patron. His audiences were transported to another place.

Throughout his career, John Eberson was hooked on selling his theatre designs. He was as adept at explaining his architectural concepts in words as he was in drawing them. To stimulate ticket sales, he described his atmospheric theatres as "wonder theatres," a term also used by the Marion Palace owner in early advertisements.

He liked adjectives. In 1926, Eberson described a new project with an exhausting explosion of them:

> *I am working on a French interpretation of an atmospheric theater—the Garden of the Tuileries. We picture a Louis sending a message through the*

> *land calling for painters, sculptors, gardeners, artisans of all kinds. And he gives the command to transform the spacious lawns lying in front of his palace into a festive ground, as he is going to entertain his grandees and dames at a glorious magic night feast.*
>
> *Months of artful effort and vast energy are devoted to the transformation and for the festive decoration of the lawns. Gigantic arches, enchanting colonnades, illuminated lattice garden houses, mystic pyrotechnic effects all silhouetted against the entrancing moonlit sky of a beautiful summer night. Surprises, illuminated fountains, music niches, lovers' lanes—a marvelous setting for a fantastic artful dance, the frills of the satin and silk-gowned nobles, the coquettish silk and ruffle-coated damsels, the air laden with the sweet perfume of jasmine.*[117]

He also understood that these designs had to generate revenue in ticket sales. His slogan reflected both of these complementary goals: "Prepare Practical Plans for Pretty Playhouses—Please Patrons—Pay Profits."[118] He called them the "nine little Ps."[119]

Every time he described his designs, his goal was to sell tickets. In doing so, he knew he would receive new commissions for more of his firm's design work. Describing the Persian atmosphere of his Avalon Theatre in Chicago, he wrote:

> *It is here that the royal nabobs and lords gather to barter and exchange everything from fruit to human souls. Behold the quietness and shade of this small pool where the numerous birds of brilliant plumage fly for refuge from the midday sun, to plunge unmolested in the clear cool water. Behold, the water carriers pause for a short siesta in the heat of the day to gaze in the pool of the Bridal Fountain and dream, perhaps—of more mysterious moonlight.*[120]

In an understatement, his daughter Elsa said of her father, "He had a great flair for the dramatic."[121]

The new style was an immediate success; in fact, it was so successful that imitators quickly surfaced. There are undocumented reports that sketches and blueprints mysteriously disappeared from his office, and that Eberson concluded that they had been stolen by competitors. Whether true or not, his design elements were included in theatres designed by other architects.

In 1926, Eberson opened an office in Midtown New York City. It was located at the Rodin Studios, 200 West Fifty-seventh Street. He made the decision to close the Chicago office in July 1929 and consolidate all of the design work in New York.[122] At about the same time, he formally brought his son, Drew (1904–1989), into the business, although Drew had helped before on many sites.[123]

Even with all of the theatre construction work, Eberson worried about overbuilding. In 1929, he advocated the remodeling of old theatres:[124]

> *More theaters—bigger theaters—better theaters—new competing chains—gigantic expansion programs—poor imitations, falling short of the mark—cheap replicas—gigantic auditoriums—lavish settings and furnishings produced and backed by the Croesuses of the modern American show business, crowd our thoughts and keep our ambitions at fever heat.*
>
> *We strive for new ideas and intelligent competitive building. Yet frenzied activities, ruled by unharnessed ambitions, are hurrying us all toward a saturation point which will soon have its telling effects on the showman on the one side and the amusement-loving public on the other.*[125]

He sensed something in the wind: America was moving too fast.

Soon after the office consolidation, the Great Depression resulted in few new theatre commissions. Like many businesses at the time, Eberson dissolved his firm in 1934.[126] Work had all but disappeared, and no economic turnaround was around the corner. The firm's seventy-two draftsmen, along with other employees, found themselves hired out to other firms or without work. For a brief time, he affiliated himself with the firm Eberson and Kautzky.

Meanwhile, Drew left for Hollywood. There, from 1935 to 1938, he found work as an uncredited assistant director for several B movies (low-budget films designed to accompany another major film in a double billing), including *Varsity Show* (1937) and *Broadway Hostess* (1935). He directed one movie, *Overland Express*, in 1938. Drew returned to New York and the architectural practice in 1938,[127] and he and his father reorganized the business under the former name of John and Drew Eberson, Architects.[128]

With demand for large atmospheric theatres nonexistent and changes in motion picture technology that favored smaller venues, Eberson began to design a different theatre. He found it in Art Deco and, later, Streamline Moderne. The popularity of these new styles reflected America's desire to overcome the Great Depression. Neon lights, vertical heights, straight lines and minimum detail all combined to create styles of architecture that looked forward, not back. Streamline Moderne architecture, with its

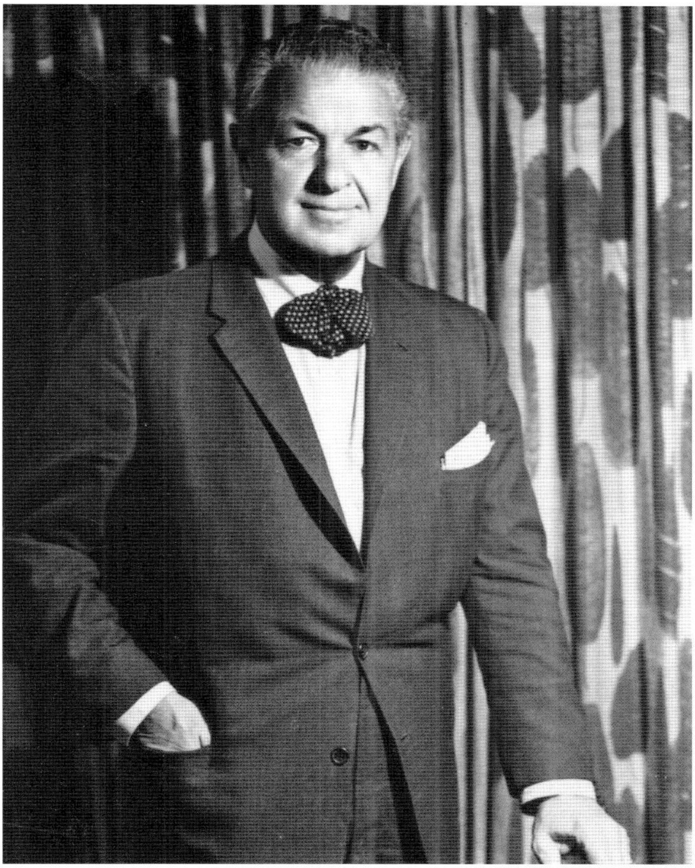

Drew Eberson, son of John Eberson. *Courtesy of the Theatre Historical Society of America.*

nautical appearance, suggested an unstoppable ship moving forward. Buildings as diverse as diners, car dealerships and dry cleaners reflected this energy. Eberson set out to capture it in new theatre designs.[129]

Eberson actually began the transition away from atmospheric theatres as early as 1930. In Mansfield, Ohio, he designed the now-demolished Warner Madison, an early Art Deco theatre.[130] Eberson didn't abandon all of his atmospheric concepts, however. In the two-thousand-seat Art Deco Auburn, New York Schines Theatre (1938), for example, foyer and lobby lights were shaped like comets and shooting stars. The auditorium had hanging stars and planets with walls that looked three-dimensional and created an impression of space.[131]

It was the Streamline Moderne style that he used more often in this period. The style employed new building and design materials, such as aluminum extrusion for railings, stainless steel and glass blocks.[132] Nothing could be more removed from the atmospheric style, yet Eberson adapted successfully. Among the theatres with this design were the Cinema Rex (Paris, 1932), the Newsreel Theatre (A.P. Building, Rockefeller Center, 1936–37) and the Lane Theatre (Staten Island, 1937–38).

The new styles also reflected a movie industry that had evolved. Convenience, comfort and safety became most important to theatre owners.[133] Concession stands, made necessary to generate additional revenue during the Depression, became standard fixtures in lobbies. The lobbies became profit centers, not elegant meeting places. Balconies were reduced to improve acoustics and sight lines. New building codes required more aisles and exits. Seating capacity was reduced by as much as half of what was required in the old atmospheric theaters.[134]

The need for master plasterers and trips to Europe to purchase Spanish furniture was gone. The proscenium arch was replaced with a large screen. Decorative plaster was replaced with acoustical panels and mirrors. "In the shortest possible time," it was observed, "Eberson's theaters had made a diametrically opposed contrast through simplicity as compared to his elaborate, cavernous, ornamented theaters of the twenties."[135]

During World War II, Eberson served on the War Production Board (WPB) Office of Civilian Requirements and was head of the theatre division.[136] An agency of the federal government, the WPB operated from 1942 to 1945. Its purpose was the regulation of production and manufacturing and the use of materials by business so that sufficient labor, material and production resources would be available for the war effort. In 1942, the WPB issued a decree that ceased all theatre construction.[137] No new theatres were built between 1942 and 1944, though some managed remodelings. The board also commandeered sound and projection equipment for the entertainment of the military.[138] "Legitimate theaters of this country have gotten along wonderfully on what little material they had on hand and there have been few if any complaints from them," Eberson told *Billboard* in 1944.[139]

In areas where the civilian workforce was involved with war production, Eberson was responsible for allocating limited entertainment resources.[140] He worked to ensure that the theatres and movie industries were seen as a necessary war industry, both for civilian and military entertainment and as a way to disseminate news and propaganda.[141] Partly due to Eberson's efforts to cause Americans to see moviegoing as patriotic, theatre attendance soared. Between 1941 and 1945, an average of eighty-five million movie tickets per year were sold.

In addition to helping with the war effort, Eberson continued his architectural work. He designed a hospital on Long Island and housing at Fort Monmouth, New Jersey, as well as at the United States Military Academy. Meanwhile, Drew Eberson was in active military service.[142]

After the war, both Ebersons reignited their architectural firm. They participated in the residential housing boom and renewed their work in theatres, both large and small. The larger theatres included the Teatro Junin in Caracas (1950) and the Teatro Roble in Mexico City (1950). In addition to theatres, Eberson also designed other buildings, such as the Niels Esperson Building (Houston).

He was active in architectural design until he could no longer work. During the later years of his life, he was fondly referred to as "Papa John" by his colleagues.[143] On March 6, 1954, John Eberson died after a long illness at the age of seventy-nine in Stamford, Connecticut.[144] After John's death in 1954, Drew directed the firm for another eighteen years.

THE STORY OF EBERSON'S life is not complete without the mention of garbage. Just as his theatre architectural practice was beginning to expand, Eberson found himself in the middle of the dirty world of Chicago politics. This chapter of his life seems completely out of character with his creative architectural career but not necessarily out of character with his salesmanship qualities. It leaves the biggest question mark about his life.

In 1906, the politically powerful Julian Syndicate from Cincinnati and Hamilton had acquired an exclusive contract to process Chicago garbage through its Chicago Reduction Company Plant. W.A. Julian, a Cincinnati shoe manufacturer, banker and political powerhouse, was the head of the syndicate. The plant had operational problems, which led to the deaths of ten workers in a 1908 naphtha explosion.[145]

After arriving in Chicago from Hamilton in 1910, Eberson was named manager of the rebuilt plant.[146] Eberson had no experience with running a garbage plant, although he apparently had developed a professional relationship with Julian.

A few weeks later, Eberson was named to an important statewide group of progressive Democrats.[147] In some cities, garbage, politics and architecture made strange bedfellows, but not in a city where building permits were tied to political contacts. He did what he had to do, and during this period Eberson was busy designing new theatres, which needed permits. One was his New Victoria Theatre, on the corner of Sheffield and Belmont in Chicago, which broke ground in October 1911.[148]

Eberson's involvement in the garbage business places an interesting twist on the reason Eberson left Hamilton or perhaps the reason he was so successful in Chicago. With success came media attention, however. His name soon became prominently featured in the *Chicago Daily Tribune*'s investigative reporting about the garbage company, including bribes, dirty tricks on political opponents and records destroyed by a mysterious fire.[149] Eventually, the city purchased the plant from the Julian Syndicate and operated the facility itself, but not before the company held the health of the city hostage while the buyout was negotiated.

Eberson didn't keep his hands out of the garbage for long.[150] In 1920, he told the *Chicago Daily Tribune* that he was offered an opportunity to purchase tankage (rendering of dead animals for use as fertilizer or feed) from the Chicago garbage stream and entered into a contract with the city.[151] The *Tribune*, noting to its readers that Eberson was an architect, questioned why the contract included a purchase price for the tankage that was significantly lower than what Eberson could sell it for in the open market. This disparity resulted in a $165,000 loss to the city.[152] The clear implication was that Eberson was redirecting city dollars to others and directly or indirectly influencing politicians. While never charged with a crime, Eberson did decide to exit the garbage business and focus on his architectural career. Why he was involved, and continued to be involved, in these activities is open to speculation. All that can be said with confidence is that Eberson was neither trained to be involved in nor had any prior experience in the garbage business.

Interestingly, in 1938, Eberson designed the Silver Theatre in Silver Spring, Maryland, just outside the District of Columbia. The theatre and adjoining shopping area were developed and owned by none other than W.A. Julian, who then served as the twenty-eighth treasurer of the United States, under Franklin D. Roosevelt.[153]

FEW PHOTOGRAPHS OF EBERSON survive. The most iconic is described by author Constance Rosenblum in her book *Boulevard of Dreams*:

> *He resembles nothing so much as a stock character from some forgotten Viennese operetta. His square face is topped by a shock of silver hair and accented by a small moustache, elfin ears, and dark brows that*

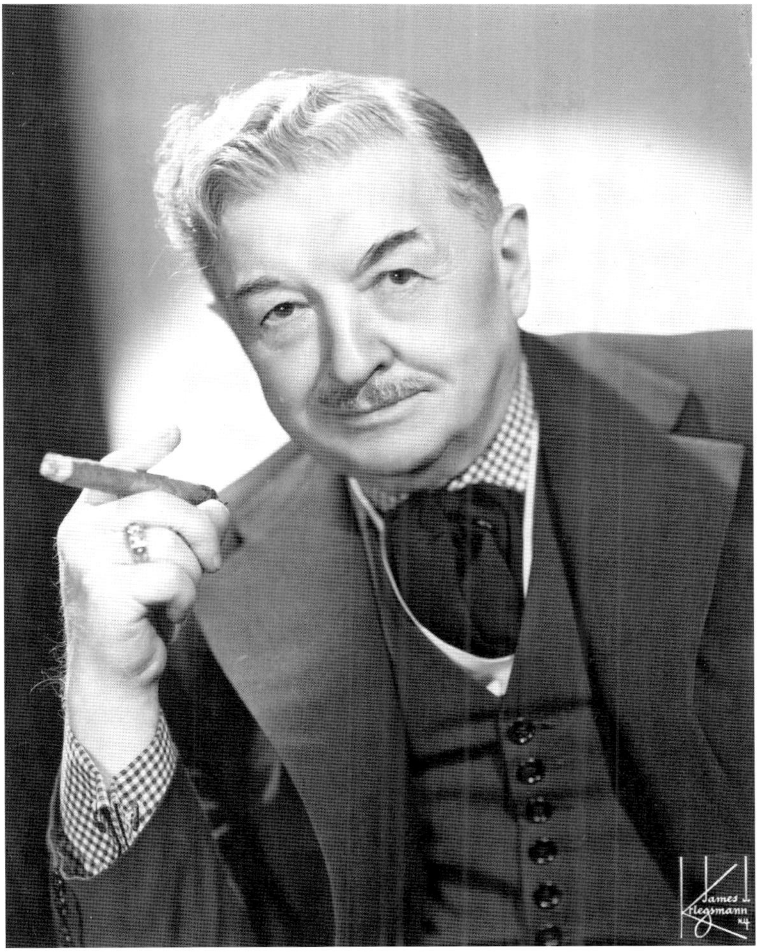

The most frequently reproduced photograph of John Eberson is this iconic portrait. *Courtesy of the Theatre Historical Society of America.*

> *shoot up at almost comical angles. A flowing four-in-hand tie peeks out of the collar of his crisp checkered shirt, the lapels of his jacket are cut uncommonly wide, a ring adorns one stubby finger, and his ever-present cigar is held at a jaunty angle.*[154]

A copy of this portrait is displayed in the Marion Palace.

In a description of Eberson in the Theatre Historical Society of America archives, his daughter Elsa described her father:

> *A little about my father's character…*[he] *never did things in an ordinary way. If he liked something he didn't buy one, he bought five or six. All special designs—car bodies, interiors, radiator hood emblems, colors, etc. Not one Chow dog (the breed he admired) but a kennel of show dogs. It was the same with horses. His clothes were all custom made and designed by him…black velvet vests with many jet buttons and white pique edging along the lapels, a brown cape with a velvet collar, black Homburg hat and flowing black artist tie. He had a strong, forceful character and when he entered a room his presence was felt—dynamic might be the word—a true showman.*

When you enter an Eberson atmospheric theatre even today, you still sense that same strong character.

4

ATMOSPHERIC THEATRES

An Acre of Seats in a Garden of Dreams

John Eberson is generally regarded as the most successful promoter of the atmospheric theatre style.[155] The design extended the stage into the entire theatre, surrounding the audience. First used commercially by him in the early 1920s, it was an instant success. In a time when theatres offered the only nonathletic entertainment venue and competition—even in small towns—was fierce, theatre developers were eager for a fresh design.

Theatre design had reached a level of predictability and boredom that no longer excited much of the public. The interiors were overstuffed and uninviting. These auditoriums groaned with fussy ornamentation, gilding and crystal chandeliers. The only thing an architect could do to try to create interest, it then seemed, was to decorate with costlier marble, larger chandeliers and even more heavily decorated domes. Some observed that while the theatres created a sense of privilege, they were now so overdone that some patrons experienced a feeling of inferiority in the opulent surroundings, which detracted from enjoyment.[156]

That changed with the atmospheric style. Rather than seating the theatre patrons in a boxlike formal setting as passive observers of stage entertainment, Eberson transported them to an exotic European courtyard or garden. A plain cerulean sky replaced the ornate dome. Wispy floating clouds produced by a projector replaced crystal chandeliers and gilt. Trees, plants, vines and taxidermy birds replaced gold leaf. Arches, trellises, balconies and plaster statuary replaced marble, painted wood panels and crystal chandeliers. As the entertainment was about to begin, lighting effects created the illusion of

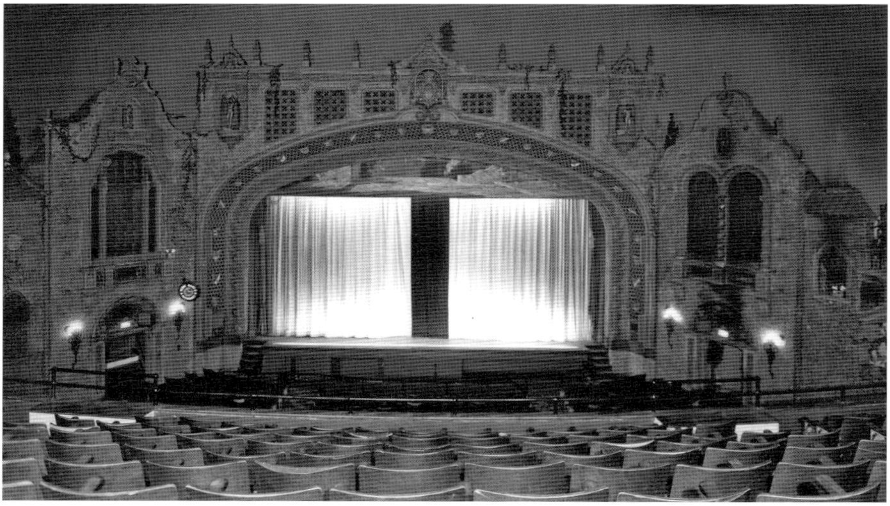

The interior of the Marion Palace Theatre. A view of the stage from the balcony, circa 1976. *Courtesy of the Palace Cultural Arts Association. Dale E. Hughes, Inc. Photography.*

a setting sun, as colors changed from yellow to red to mauve. Small lights, arranged in the ceiling in constellation patterns, twinkled to create a sense of infinite space. Eberson made the theatre patron an active, comfortable resident of an imaginary time and place, not a passive, aloof occupant of an oppressive formal space.

While Eberson had the most commercial success with the atmospheric style, there were predecessors. Architect John Pridmore designed the Cort Theatre (Chicago, 1908) as an outdoor amphitheatre, complete with a sky painted with stars and a moon viewed through a trellis with hanging vines. Even earlier, the New Theatre (Philadelphia, 1794) had a ceiling painted like a daytime sky, as did numerous eighteenth-century opera houses.

The atmospheric concept had entered the imagination of architects centuries earlier. Born in Europe, Eberson traveled extensively in France, Spain and Italy[157] and may have been influenced by the Teatro Olimpico in Vicenza, Italy. Andrea Palladio (1508–1580) began its construction in 1580, just before his death. Completed in 1585 by Vincenzo Scamozzi, it is still in use as a theatre. Inside, theatre patrons are transported to an Italian Renaissance courtyard where a half circle of tiered seats (benches) surrounds the stage. A courtyard is simulated by a colonnade with statues that surround and are behind the audience. The ceiling is painted blue, suggesting an open sky. Eberson never mentioned Teatro Olimpico in his known writings, so it is nothing more than somewhat informed speculation to conclude that he was influenced by it.

Few of John Eberson's writings survive. One that does is the advertising piece, veiled as a news article, that he wrote for *Motion Picture News*. It is useful because Eberson discusses his ideas and design techniques for atmospheric theatres.[158] Eberson gives credit to William A. Johnston, editor of *Motion Picture News*, for the idea to deviate from traditional theatre architectural style and develop something new. He was persuaded by Johnston's belief that it is the goal of a modern showman to provide an audience with a "warm and friendly atmosphere" to make them feel at home and a part of the show.

According to Eberson's son, Drew, his father believed that the ornate movie palaces "were gradually being overdone and had become static in design."[159] "To be a successful theatre architect," wrote John Eberson, "one must be a showman—of this I was convinced."[160] Traditional theatre architecture was neither warm nor friendly. For Eberson, the architecture basically copied historical buildings, opera houses and grand palaces in European cities and had become distracting and oppressive. The country was saturated with them, and Eberson, the showman, set out to develop something new.

At the same time that Eberson looked for new ideas, theatre exhibitors had become weary of the high cost of building these traditional, overly ornamented theatres. Wages for ornamental plasterers, for example, hit an all-time high as post–World War I construction demand increased.[161] Eberson saw that the expense of some new theatres was beyond what could be justified from ticket receipts. To pay for the building, the exhibitor had little choice other than to book expensive talent, which then raised admission prices to the point where the theatre lost its most important and lucrative following: the family trade.

While there is some good-natured debate about which theatre became the first to open with the new Eberson atmospheric style, Eberson himself credited the Hoblitzelle Majestic Theatre (Houston, 1923) as the first.[162] Clearly, Eberson tried out some of his concepts at the Orpheum Theatre (Wichita, 1922). However, with the Majestic, he built on those and added many others to define his style and make the departure from all that came before. With the Majestic, Eberson became part architect, part set designer. The designs were, in his words, "a form and style that represented something new, but which was imbued with character and individuality."[163]

The Majestic was designed as an Italian piazza. The exterior had a neoclassical brick façade, giving the illusion of a building in Rome. It even included a frieze of dancers and musicians. Inside, Eberson created a classical Roman garden. It had asymmetrical walls with building façades of different types and dimensions. Windows and balconies were lighted from inside to mimic life indoors. Roofs were topped with simulated tiles. Artificial vines and trees were placed realistically. Even papier-mâché doves were suspended to appear as if they were in flight. The ceiling was painted a dark blue to resemble a nighttime sky and was banked with blue lights to create the glow of a twilight horizon. Openings were placed strategically in the ceiling and outfitted with twinkling lights to resemble stars. Moving clouds were projected on the ceiling. Before a performance, orange lights along the ceiling were increased and then dimmed to simulate a sunset. The final touches included an airplane passing through the sky, a recording of nighttime noises and a rising moon. Nothing like this had ever been tried before.

In addition to the atmospheric design innovation, the floor plan was equally innovative for the time. It was a square plan, not a long rectangle common in other theatres. The balcony was deep, extending over half of the orchestra-level seats. This plan allowed each seat to have a maximum focal line, for both the stage and the surrounding walls.[164]

Architects Celeste Williams and Dietmar Forehlich have explained the design innovation:

> *Eberson's innovation was his asymmetrical balance of harmonic elements to the right and left of the stage. Digressing from the norm of exactly balancing elements to control acoustics, Eberson's enhanced the authenticity of the atmospheric experience by weighting the Roman Palace theater organ grilles on the proscenium left to balance the Italian Terrace and statuary on the right.*
>
> *He discovered that there was no discernible change in acoustical integrity and opened the path for an instinctive approach to visual arrangement that broke with rigid symmetry. This method of arranging spatial groups, when combined with projecting tiered box seating, realistic transitional architectural elements between buildings and sky, and side and rear under-balcony (parterre) sculpture, provided the sensation of being surrounded by the theater—one felt as if one were part of the staging. The fantasy and exoticism the patrons saw in the films were reflected in the theater.*[165]

A sense of being surrounded by the theatre was just as important as the individual design elements. Without that sense of space, Eberson's innovation would have fallen flat.

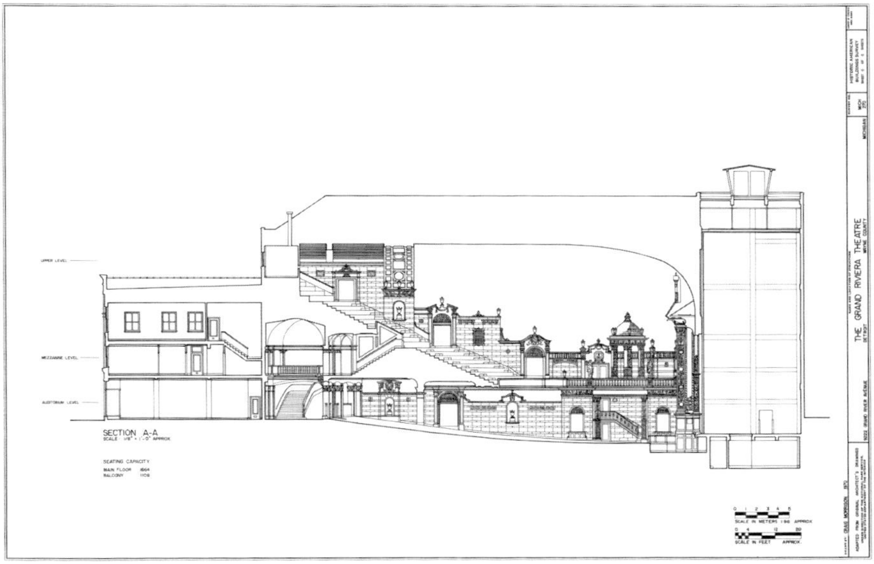

Elevation plans for the Grand Riviera Theatre in Detroit, adapted from Eberson's original drawings. *Courtesy of the Library of Congress.*

Eberson continued this asymmetrical design in all of his atmospheric theatres. There is no repetition, which would destroy the illusion. The scale of the buildings is small by design to achieve the effect that they are far away. Different sized statuary is used at different heights to maximize the effect of distance. Finally, the degree of projection of the building features away from the theatre walls completes the illusion of outdoor space.[166]

He attributed the success of his design style to the uniqueness of it. However, he described it as merely imitating, in a dignified way, "nature glorifying classic architecture."[167] He seemed surprised with the success. "Few innovations in the theatrical business," he wrote, "have taken root as quickly as the Atmospheric Theatre."[168]

His style reflected a change in the use of theatres. Program variety—opera, vaudeville, motion pictures—necessitated a theatre interior style that would not compete with the program on the stage. For Eberson, an outdoor setting was the answer, although it was a difficult design. He described it this way:

> *We find it more difficult to design and execute a genuine "atmospheric" theatre than what we term a "formal" theatre. The necessary amount of detail work and study to create a consistent atmospheric theatre is endless. It is true—we are*

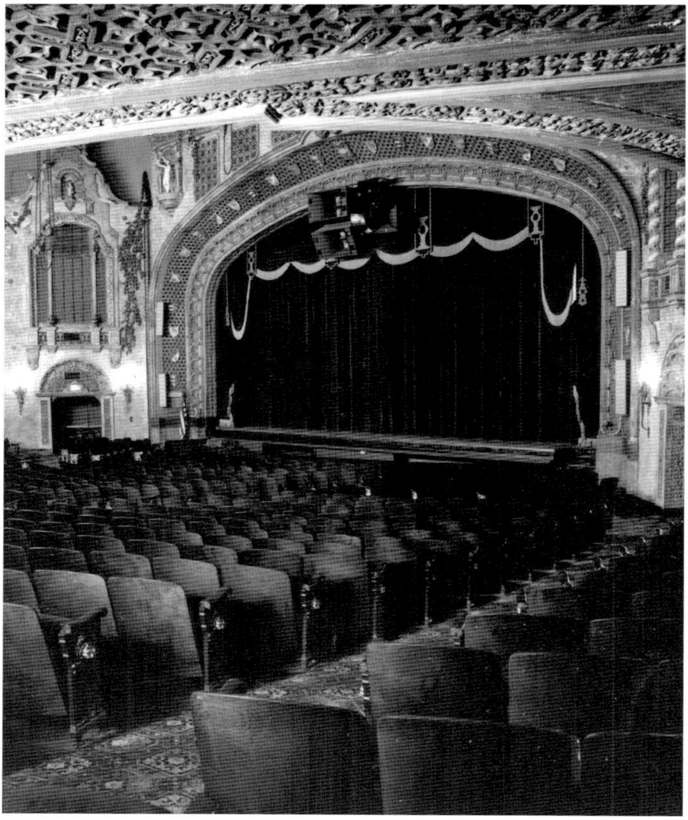

Left: The interior of the Marion Palace Theatre. A view from the orchestra section, under the balcony, circa 1976. *Courtesy of the Palace Cultural Arts Association. Dale E. Hughes, Inc. Photography.*

Below: The interior of the Marion Palace Theatre. A view of a portion of the east wall, circa 1976. *Courtesy of the Palace Cultural Arts Association. Dale E. Hughes, Inc. Photography.*

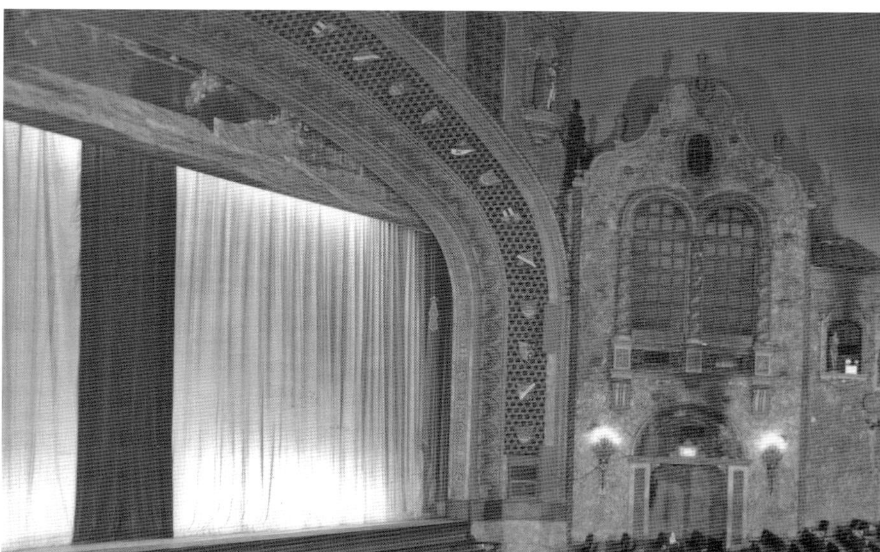

> *glorifying classic architecture and form, but to make the illusion perfect requires not only a thorough understanding and knowledge of old world architecture, but we must also know how to transform and create these antique soft textured and interestingly polychromed buildings with modern tools and artcraft…*
>
> *To be really successful, and not just an imitator copying the work of others, we must historically, graphically and architecturally study the periods and old world localities which are furnishing the theme for our outdoor garden auditoriums.*[169]

In an outdoor setting, Eberson believed that theatre patrons could relax, surrounded by natural beauty. That comfort could not be found in the cold grandeur of other theatres.

Color selection was important in an Eberson atmospheric theatre, and he believed it set his theatres apart from those of his competitors. Eberson said that "the very nature of the pastel coloring executed in hundreds of desired shades and colors, lends itself so well to the imagination of the average person, and as we linger and look about, our fancy is free to conjure endless tales of romance."[170] He favored blue, orange and myrtle green. Nut browns and grays were used for walls because of their ability to take artificial light. He did not decorate the walls with red, which he considered a very unlucky color for a theatre, unless it was for carpeting. He also avoided gold and purple.[171]

Eberson worked very hard to capture the blue color of a twilight sky, a trademark of all his theatres. He explained the color in the *Motion Picture News* article:

> *Did you ever notice the peculiar blue we are now using in our atmospheric theatres? It releases the nerve tension of the audience; refreshes the eye, makes one feel that one can breathe, and it has one hundred and one beneficial effects on the mind and nerves.*
>
> *Blue is always described as the color of Hope. This is not a fanciful and trivial sentiment, but a fact which can be scientifically proved, but it must be a certain, defined and distinct blue on a certain defined and distinct textured surface. We know how to do this, but cannot write specifications to cover the execution of this "Color Health Recipe."*[172]

Thus, the texture of the finish plaster coat, together with the blue color used, combined to create the illusion of the sky.

Relief colors and highlight colors were equally important to his designs. Indeed, today, one of the most difficult things to replicate in an

Eberson theatre is the precise color scheme. Drew Eberson later recalled the painting technique:

> *We used tempera paint, red, green and brown in big globs, smeared it around with a rag until we got the right effect and then lacquered over it. We used pure hues, raw colors. We had to. They were seen in the subdued light of the theatre and needed a lot of punch to show up.*[173]

In an advertisement for his Michael Angelo Studios, Eberson recognized that most of the time, audiences would see his work in the dark: "CINEMAS MUST HAVE DECORATIONS TO BE SEEN AND FELT IN THE DARK."[174] It was a process so exacting that, rather than using local painters, all of the interior painting work was done by the thirty people who made up the Michael Angelo design team. They traveled from theatre to theatre to complete Eberson's vision.[175]

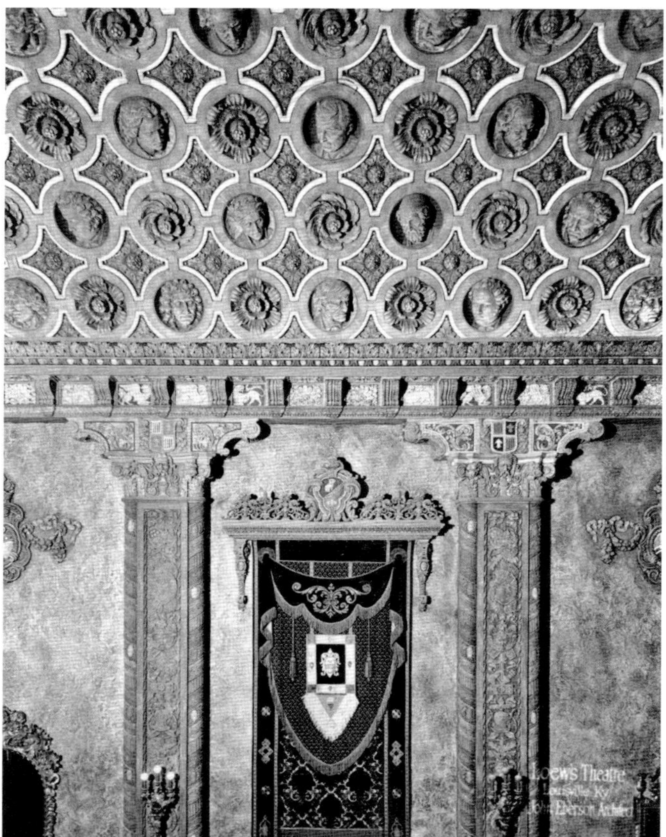

The decoration of Eberson's theatres was largely the responsibility of his family. His wife, Beatrice, and their daughter Elsa made the banners, like this one in the Palace Theatre in Louisville, Kentucky. *Courtesy of the Library of Congress.*

He also attributed his firm's success to the "minutest" attention to detail and consistency in the execution of the work. Eberson wrote in *Motion Picture News* that "[we] have to be sculptors—we have to be designers—detailers, decorators, lighting engineers and connoisseurs of fine furniture, soft fabrics and correct bric-a-brac."[176] The "proper furnishings" for an atmospheric theatre were found in the antique market or antique reproduction market. None of the expensive, gaudy and elaborate bric-a-brac required for a formal theatre was needed for an Eberson.

Heating and cooling systems were also treated in what he called a warm and friendly way. By this, Eberson meant that the exposed grills were antiqued metals that fit with the design. Gone were the shiny, polished brass grills that were expensive to purchase and maintain.

The entire theatre design was executed in a way that left room for *imagination*. His designers and decorators were taught "the art of appealing to the imagination of the public, and whenever you leave something to your imagination, you automatically and instantaneously create interest."[177] All of the plans, designs, colors, lighting effects, statues and furnishings in an Eberson atmospheric theatre left open room for imagination. Patrons might find an empty balcony window, the shape of a constellation (in the Marion Palace, the Big Dipper on the ceiling is reproduced, and Polaris is in the correct position, pointing north) or a flying pigeon, all of which can tell many different stories.

The auditorium of the theatre was not the only place that received Eberson's atmospheric treatment. Lobbies, restrooms and even nursery rooms were included. In the San Antonio Majestic, for example, a nursery was provided for the children of patrons. It had a cobalt blue Vitrolite-tiled washroom and a playroom with fairy tale murals, stained-glass windows and a floor with animal designs.[178] This attention to detail and comfort earned high customer satisfaction and repeat patronage.[179]

Eberson understood that the atmospheric design did not guarantee success for a theatre owner. In a *Motion Picture News* article, Eberson wrote that he wanted to create a space that was cost-effective and comfortable.[180] An Eberson atmospheric theatre cost about one-fourth the amount of a standard theatre.[181] He attributed the savings to less bronze, marble and hangings. In *Motion Picture News*, he explained, "We strive to use more art and less tedious methods of decorating to get our effects. Our appropriation for lighting fixtures which are usually either imported originals or true copies of foreign characteristic work, is smaller than required for palatial formal interiors."[182]

Part of the savings came from the plasterwork. Ben Hall, author of *Best Remaining Seats*, explained:

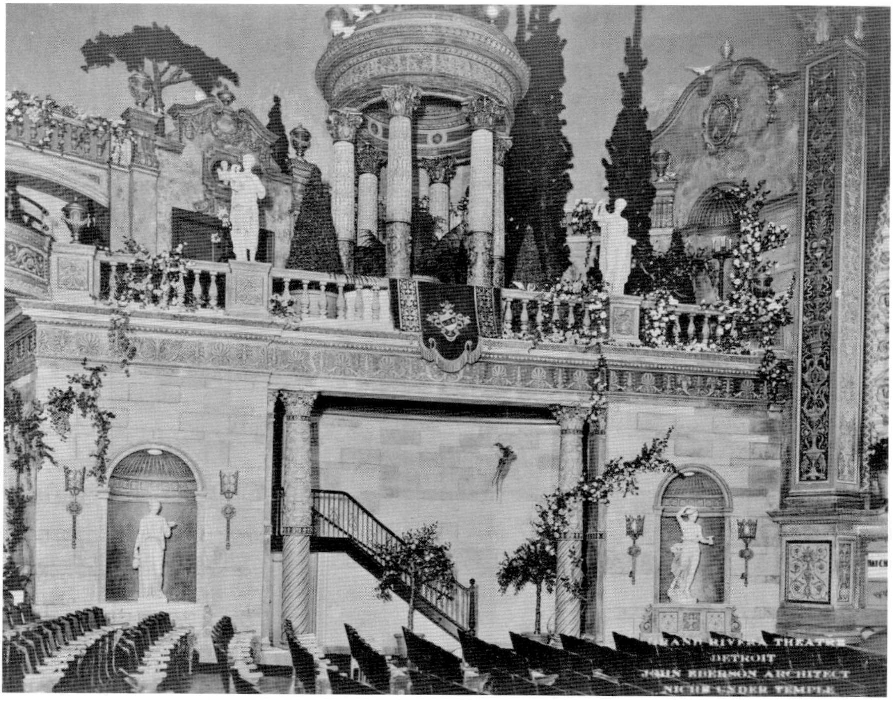

A view of the Grand Riviera Theatre in Detroit. Eberson often used a macaw as his artistic signature, as found here at the bottom of the stairway. In the Marion Palace, the macaw is located in a west wall archway. *Courtesy of the Library of Congress.*

> *The simple plaster vault of the ceiling, with its projected clouds and handful of low-wattage stars, was economical in comparison with classic domes, ornamental beams, stupendous chandeliers. Most of Eberson's decorative details—gazebos, trellises, columns, arches, cherubim and seraphim—were made of cast-plaster. And many stock models of these items popped up time after time in Eberson atmospherics around the country, differing only in the peacocks they supported or the amount of arbutus that trailed around them.*[183]

For theatre owners, Eberson's appeal was only partly aesthetic; the huge construction savings and ongoing public appeal were paramount benefits.

The design could be scaled up or down, based on the lot size, number of competitors and the local population. Eberson said in a *Motion Picture News* article that there was a large demand for small theatres in small towns.[184] His firm had developed several plans for low-cost atmospheric theatres in these places. The Marion Palace was one. Rather than a $1 million construction price tag, the Marion Palace was designed, built, decorated and furnished (including retail spaces) for half that amount.

In part, he was able to provide cost savings by supplying much of the interior decorating work through the company that he and his wife created, Michael Angelo Studios. This caused some ethical issues for him, but the risk of self-dealing was, in his view, overridden by the control it gave him over the decorating of his theatres and the savings he could provide to clients by dealing directly with suppliers. While he operated Michael Angelo Studios with a profit motive, the artistic control it gave him far outweighed, in his mind, any ethical problem of directing work to a business he owned.[185] It was difficult to find skilled artisans in each town where a theatre was constructed who possessed adequate skills to carry out Eberson's specifications.

Much of the interior was actually prefabricated and shipped to the construction site. This not only lowered the fabrication costs but also allowed Eberson to further reduce costs by using pieces designed for one theatre in another theatre design miles away.[186] Also, it was not practical to pour plaster into rubber molds and allow for curing time at the job site.

Each plaster piece (or set piece, as Eberson called them) was labeled and carefully packed for shipment by rail. On arrival, Eberson's own skilled craftsmen, not local laborers, uncrated the pieces and assembled them according to detailed plans. These craftsmen were also responsible for installation of the final effects, such as trees, ivy and taxidermy birds.[187]

He did not fabricate everything, however. In addition to furniture and light fixtures, which he often acquired in Europe, New York and New Orleans, Eberson purchased the sculpture reproductions from the Boston firm of P.P. Caproni and Brother.[188] The firm was so highly regarded in Europe that the Caproni brothers were sometimes the only men allowed to take castings of original sculptures. Yet the craftsmanship was not reflected in the prices. An eight-foot-high reproduction cost less than $100.

The atmospheric theatre was an illusion—Eberson's illusion—and became America's illusion. Clients included the Young Amusement Company, which built the Marion Palace Theatre; Loew's; Paramount; Universal; and Warner Brothers. By the end of the 1920s, Eberson had designed more than 160 theatres in the United States, England, France, Australia and New Zealand, over 100 of which were atmospheric theatres.[189] His style was replicated in England by such architects as Leathart and Granger, who modeled some theatres on the Eberson style, as did Edward Stone and T.R. Sumerford.[190] In Paris, Eberson collaborated on the Rex, France's first atmospheric theatre, which was designed by P. Beuysen.[191] Even other American theatre architects

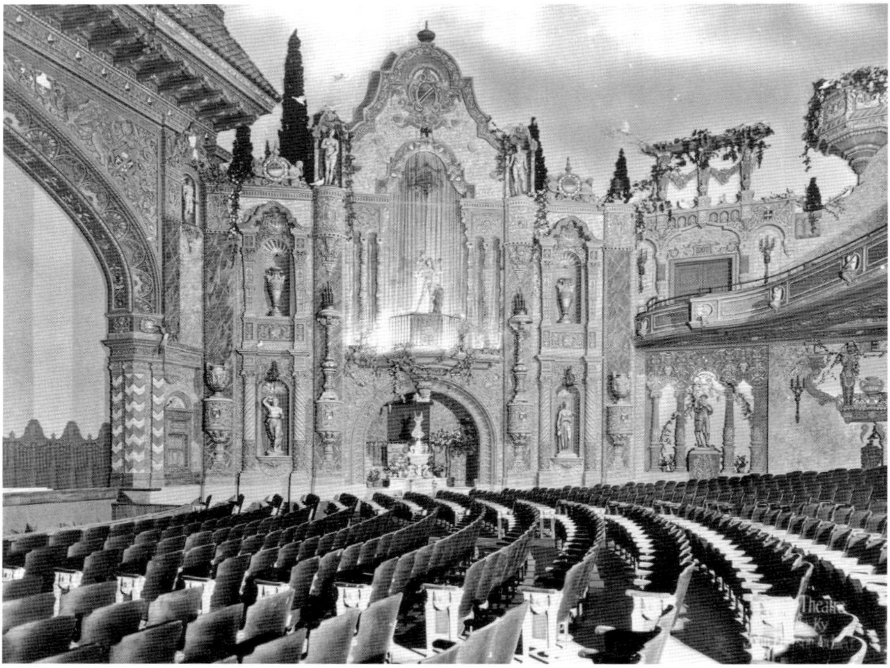

An interior view of the Palace Theatre in Louisville, Kentucky. The Spanish Baroque, Churriguerresque-motif theatre opened two days after the Marion Palace Theatre, on September 1, 1928. *Courtesy of the Library of Congress.*

eventually designed atmospheric theatres, at client request. The most famous of these were Rapp and Rapp and Thomas Lamb.[192]

Not everyone was a fan, however, particularly in the architectural community.[193] One observer wrote:

> *This irresponsible reproduction of all the great architectural treasures of the ages so cheapens public taste that one wonders if a whole generation is not now arising whose artistic appreciation will be so warped that in years to come, Americans visiting the great sites of antiquity will be heard to remark: "So this is the Taj Mahal; pshaw…the Oriental Theatre at home is twice as big and has electric lights besides."*[194]

Some architects did not want to accept that American consumerism was reshaping almost all aspects of American life, including the design of buildings.

P. Morton Shand, an Englishman who was critical of the American movie industry, was equally disapproving of Eberson's theatres. In 1930, Shand wrote that atmospheric theatres were "like nauseating stick-jaw candy, so fulsomely flavoured with the syrupy romanticism of popular novels and the 'see Naples and die' herd-nostalgia."[195]

Despite the criticism, this type of exotic architecture succeeded because Americans wanted it. They experienced it in movies, at world fairs and in the travel writings of the adventurer Richard Halliburton. Eventually, they wanted it in their homes, as developers promoted English Tudor–style cottages and Spanish-style haciendas.[196] It did not matter that these theatres and houses were only illusions with their plaster finishes and mass-produced wrought-iron railings. It gave them an escape from whatever disillusionment rested uncomfortably under the surface of their lives.

Atmospheric design fell out of favor with the start of the Great Depression, as almost all capital for new construction evaporated. Motion pictures began to change and with them the interest in atmospherics. While an atmospheric theatre worked with the sheiks, Latin lovers and faraway settings of the movies of the 1920s, that style of design made less sense when those themes departed the screen in the 1930s. By then, the dark days ahead had made the exotic unattainable, even in dreams.

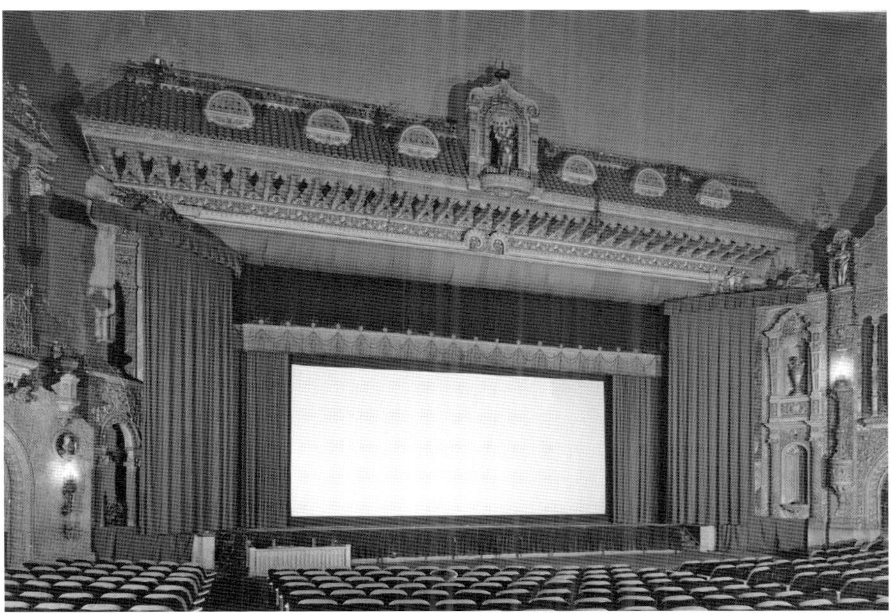

A view of the proscenium stage at the Palace Theatre in Louisville, Kentucky. Note the transition from the heavily decorated sidewalls to the stage, a transition aided by the red tile roof at the top of the stage. *Courtesy of the Library of Congress.*

Table 1

JOHN EBERSON ATMOSPHERIC THEATERS IN OPERATION IN THE UNITED STATES

Theatre	Location	Style	Interesting Features	Opened	Restored
Majestic	Dallas, TX	Renaissance Revival	Bird-cage elevator served balconies	1921	1983
Orpheum	Wichita, KS	Spanish Courtyard	Original asbestos fire curtain still in use	1922	1984
Indiana	Terre Haute, IN	Spanish Courtyard	Lobby fitted with thirty-eight statues	1922	2013
Avalon	Chicago	Moorish Revival	Lobby has five murals made with tiny inlaid mosaic tiles	1925	2008
Palace	Canton, OH	Spanish Courtyard	Original Kilgen theatre organ still in use	1926	1980
Tampa	Tampa, FL	Florida Mediterranean/ Spanish	First air-conditioned building in Tampa	1926	1977
Olympia	Miami, FL	Moorish	Taxidermy peacock on display—an Eberson trademark	1926	1975
State	Kalamazoo, MI	Spanish Courtyard	Original Barton theatre organ still in use	1927	1985
Riviera (Rose Blumkin)	Omaha, NE	Hispano-Italian	Water fountains and goldfish	1927	1990s
Palace	Marion, OH	Spanish Courtyard	A statue of George Washington is found in the balcony	1928	1975
Palace	Louisville, KY	Spanish Baroque	Opening day movie was *Excess Baggage*—just like the Marion Palace	1928	1981
Uptown	Kansas City, MO	Mediterranean Courtyard	Mechanical birds	1928	1994
Loews (Carpenter)	Richmond, VA	Spanish-Moorish	Entrance lobby wraps around corner of building	1928	1993
Paramount	Anderson, IN	Spanish Courtyard	Original Page organ still in use	1929	1995
Civic	Akron, OH	Moorish and Mediterranean	Entrance lobby extends over Ohio and Erie Canal	1929	2000
Majestic	San Antonio	Spanish Courtyard	Goldfish aquarium	1929	1989

PART IV
BUILDING A PALACE

5

THE SITE AND CONSTRUCTION

The Palace site was purchased by the Young Amusement Company on August 18, 1927, a little over a year before the theatre opened.[197] Purchase terms had been agreed to a month earlier, on June 18.[198] V.U. Young and C.J. Wolf, together with Canton, Ohio investors Edward E. Bender and Sol Bernstein, met at the Harding Hotel to finish the deal on behalf of Young Amusement Company.[199]

The site was 120 feet wide and 153 feet deep, fronting on West Center and Campbell Streets.[200] A corner lot on a busy street, it was a perfect site for a theatre. Like other commercial buildings constructed in a growing town, it was surrounded by a mixture of buildings, in this case the Central Junior High School, Harding Hotel and residences.

Local realtors J.W. Thew and R.T. Lewis and businessman David W. Evans (owner of a limestone company and a realty company) actively lobbied Young and Wolf to place a theatre in Marion.[201] In addition to civic pride, each hoped his real estate interests would increase in value if a new theatre were constructed. The local owners of Harding Hotel also helped convince the company to locate a theatre in Marion.[202]

The decision to build the Palace on West Center Street began simply enough. Young Amusement Company representatives were brought to Marion by Thew to examine a lot for a theatre.[203] Dissatisfied with it but intrigued with Marion, the representatives stayed to examine other sites. They were most interested in the vacant lot on West Center Street that was directly across from the Harding Hotel.[204] Already convinced of the value of the lot for commercial development, Lewis held an option on it.[205] He had planned to earn a hefty commission by selling the lot for a filling station.[206] He dropped this development effort, however, when it became clear that a theatre at this site would be much better for Marion and development on West Center Street.[207]

The site was owned by George D. Copeland and Katherine Bartram Copeland, who lived immediately west of the planned site at 282 West Center Street. Their home was on the site now occupied by the Palace Pavilion addition. George Copeland was an attorney who practiced for a period with John H. Bartram and, later, with Hayes Thompson. Copeland died in May 1928, before the Palace opened.

The site consisted of two large lots. There was no building on the corner lot, which had been vacant for many years.[208] To the immediate west was a lot with a two-story frame house that would be razed.[209] The Copelands would remain in their home and have the Palace as a new neighbor.[210]

The Copelands were represented in the negotiations by Evans and Lewis.[211] According to the *Marion Star*, neither received compensation for their work other than the indirect benefit that a theatre would provide to their real estate interests on West Center Street.[212] The price paid for the theatre site was undisclosed.

Two years after the Palace opened, a dispute occurred about the money Young Amusement Company owed Katherine Copeland. A $150,000 foreclosure action was brought by Katherine and her daughter against the company. It is likely that this was the purchase price for the site, represented by $150,000 in notes they held. Their foreclosure alleged that the mortgage was breached when motion picture sound equipment was added to the Palace. John H. Bartram successfully represented the company, and the case was dismissed.[213] An eight-foot strip of land along the west side of the lot was sold by the Copelands to the Young company for $5,000 just three days after the foreclosure was dismissed, suggesting that a settlement of the dispute had been reached.

That was not the only problem the Young Amusement Company encountered with the site. Both Young and Eberson would have liked more land to the north. It was needed to allow for a deeper stage, greater stage access on the west and more seats. However, the Harrold family, owners of the lot (131 Campbell Street), refused to sell. They also owned an automobile service and repair business behind the Palace. To relocate their home and the business would be an inconvenience they did not want to bear without a large premium.

Rather than make the stage smaller with a perfect rectangular shape, the Palace stage was built as designed and then angled southwest in the stage area behind the light board and fly walk. The total seats did not decrease below the 1,500 planned. Years later, the northern lot was acquired for the Palace from Jerry Northrup and is today used as a parking lot.

Work between Young and Eberson on the architectural plans began in July 1927, just after the new theatre was announced in the *Marion Star*.[214] While no complete construction records survive, Drew Eberson summarized the typical construction routine in a 1989 interview:

> *From the day the contract was signed until the theatre opened, countless people were involved. The drawings themselves came from the initial sketches. They took about two months to complete with 40 or 50 people working on them. It was a huge task.*
>
> *Sometimes area architects were hired to get us by the local inspectors, but most of the time Father controlled the entire operation through our own supervisor. A local contractor was selected by competitive bids. It was hard to turn over a complete job to a regular architect or contractor, theatre building being as specialized as it is. For instance a steel beam can be somewhat flexible in other buildings, but if an audience feels the slightest movement in a balcony they are panicky. We strengthened the span and tested the load capacity carefully with sandbags until it was completely stable.*
>
> *Father visited the sites once a month usually, by train, lodging at the local hotel. During the peak of the atmospheric theatre boom he was on the road most of the time. When construction began, his own group of specialists moved in to complete the building with help from local workers. About thirteen months later we had a theatre opening.*[215]

The "specialists" were all employees of Eberson's design company, Michael Angelo Studios, whose job it was to complete the unique painting, furnishing and installation work that made an atmospheric theatre complete.

Excavation work started on October 31, 1927, by Drake & Sons of Marion, just a week after it was awarded the contract.[216] Drake was also responsible for the foundation work.[217] An Osgood steam shovel was used for the excavation, which was expected to be completed in fifteen days.[218] Poor weather delayed the completion, however, and work continued into December.[219]

Like many theatres, the excavation plan was to grade the ground on a slope leading down to the orchestra pit.[220] This allowed for the proper incline for the 1,540 seats (today there are 1,420 seats). A twelve-foot-deep basement

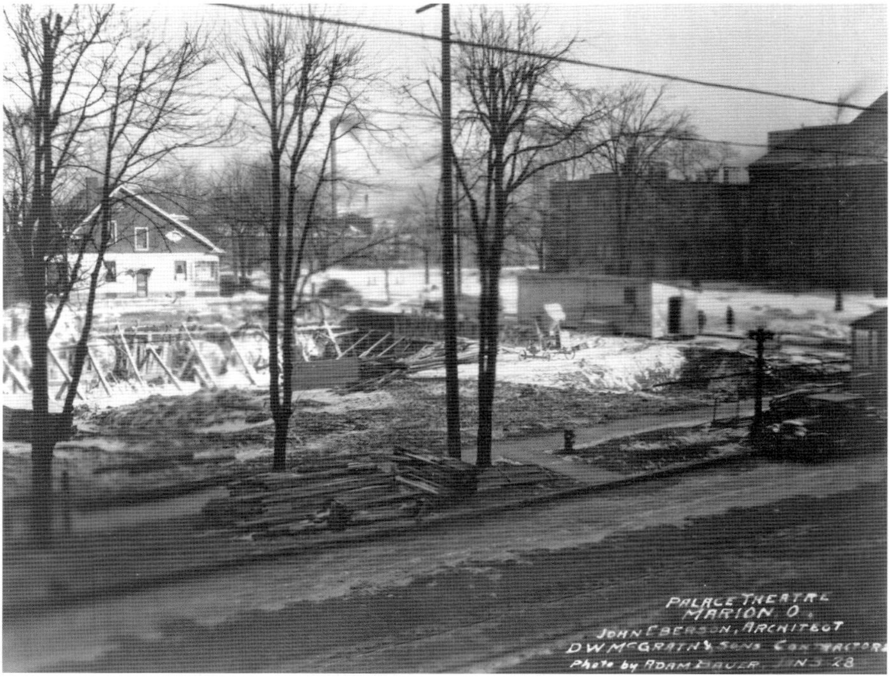

This photo shows the progress of excavation work on January 3, 1928. To the right is Central Junior High School. The house at the back belonged to the Harrold family, who refused to sell their land for the theatre. *Courtesy of the Marion County Historical Society.*

was excavated at the southeast corner for the Palace's storage, and another basement, eighteen feet deep, was dug at the rear of the building, parallel to West Center Street, for the heating and cooling plant.[221] Excavated soil was used to fill railroad land at a location a short distance from Campbell Street, and any extra was to be used at the Marion Cemetery.[222]

The construction contract was signed on December 23, 1927, with D.W. McGrath & Sons of Columbus. The construction price was $300,000, not including the site cost, site preparation or equipment, which made the total price $500,000.[223]

The contract contemplated the construction of a three-story building facing West Center Street, with a higher stage elevation in back. In addition to the theatre, the contractor agreed to build two-story extensions for retail shops, storerooms and residential apartments on the first and second floors. The small third floor would house the projection room. It would be built using steel, concrete, brick and stone and finished with terra cotta and polychrome. A three-story lobby was included in the original plans but was later redesigned to maximize rental space on the second floor.[224]

In announcing the construction contract, Young took the opportunity to describe the interior of the theatre to the *Marion Star*:

> *In describing the theatre plans, Mr. Young says that although the entire structure is to be of unusual beauty, the outstanding attraction will be the auditorium, which will represent a Spanish garden on a moonlight night with tiny stars twinkling in the sky and fleecy clouds floating overhead. The sides of the auditorium will be designed to picture flower-bedecked garden walls.*
>
> *Indirect lighting will be used throughout the auditorium. Wall lamps and floor lamps will also add to the beauty and dignity of the theatre, which Mr. Young says may be best described as "A Spanish Castle" or "A Palace in Old Spain."*
>
> *"The auditorium and stage lighting schemes include the very latest in plans for effect," Mr. Young states. "The lighting effect will give the interior of the playhouse added beauty and an individuality possessed by no other theater in the state."*
>
> *Furnishings of the theatre are to be of high standard and costly design to harmonize with the general plans, Mr. Young says.*
>
> *It is also announced that conforming with a policy to present a program to include vaudeville, motion pictures and legitimate attractions, a stage adequate for the largest productions is planned by the architect. The stage equipment is to include all of the latest devices for mechanical and lighting effects.*
>
> *Dressing rooms are to be large, well-ventilated and lighted. Shower and tub baths and many other conveniences are incorporated in the plans for the comfort of performers.*
>
> *The orchestra pit will be large enough to accommodate a symphony concert orchestra, while the organ console will be located at one side of the pit.*
>
> *Special attention, Mr. Young states, will be given to ventilating, heating and cooling systems, the builders recognizing these as some of the most important factors in theatre construction.*
>
> *The latest type of projection machines will be installed to assure perfect screening of motion pictures, it is announced.*[225]

Young's summary shows the depth of construction work involved in the eight-month project.

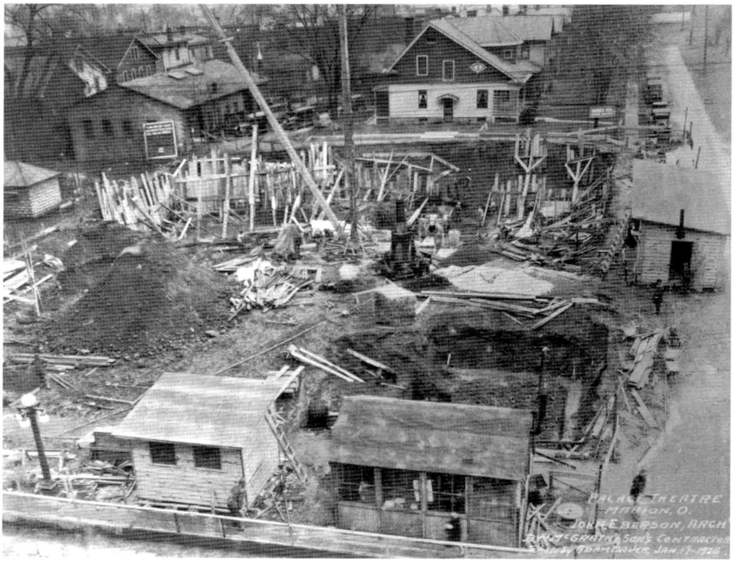

As the weather improved, excavation work could continue, as shown here on January 17, 1928. The areas below the stage were excavated, wooden supports were being erected and the footers were beginning to be poured. *Courtesy of the Marion County Historical Society.*

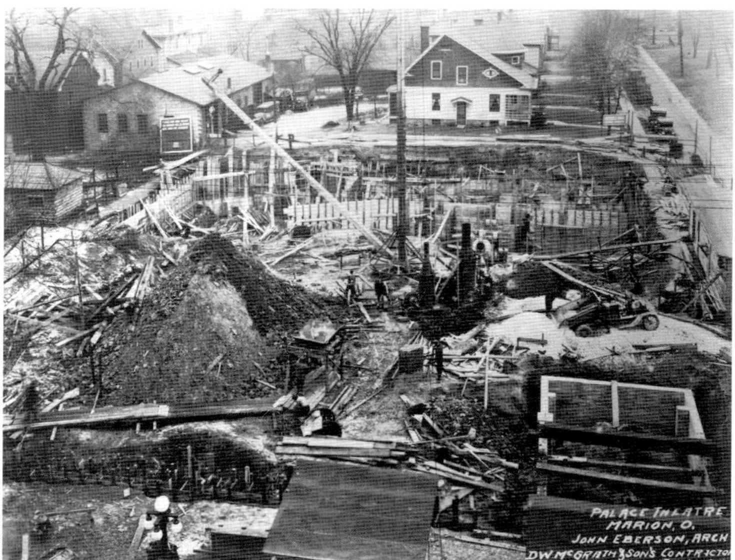

By February 1, 1928, foundation work had progressed, including the laying of foundation blocks for the basement at the southeast corner. *Courtesy of the Palace Cultural Arts Association.*

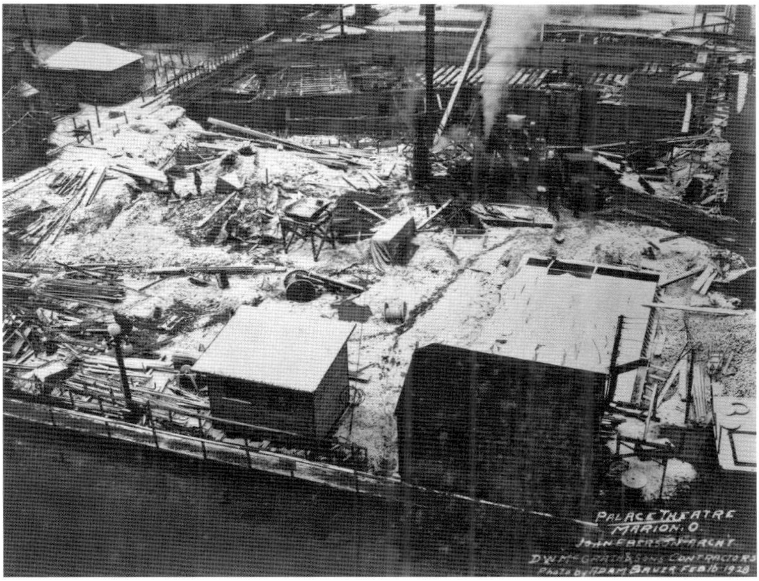

Work to pour the basement floor under the stage area had begun by February 16, 1928. This level would hold the ventilation and heating systems. *Courtesy of the Marion County Historical Society.*

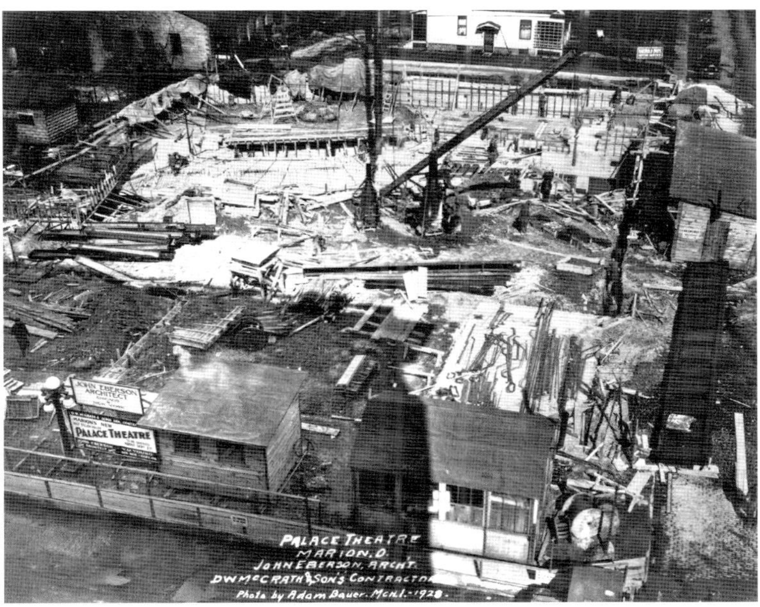

Concrete work on the basement levels was complete on March 1, 1928. *Courtesy of the Palace Cultural Arts Association.*

On February 23, 1928, concrete work began for the second floor of the basement. Work on the first floor of the basement, which would hold the heating plant and storage, was already complete. The new concrete work made the ceiling of the first floor of the basement and what would become the floor for the second floor of the basement. The second floor of the basement would be finished to contain the dressing rooms and the understage corridor that allows passage of actors and stagehands from stage left to stage right, unseen by the audience. Immediately above the second floor of the basement would be the stage. Work was also underway to place the forms for the rear and sidewalls of the basement.[226]

After a delay caused by a heavy snowfall, work on the Palace continued rapidly. On March 8, the *Marion Star* reported that some of the steel had been erected on the West Center Street side of the theatre. Also, bricklayers were laying hollow tile for the rear and sidewalls, and dark brick was being laid on the outside wall. Concrete work had been completed on the stage and the foundation, with the exception of the south end of the east wall. Work moved quickly, helped in part by excellent construction weather.[227] By June, the exterior of the building was almost complete, and work inside the building could begin to reach completion. By mid-August, only finishing work remained.

Heating and ventilation equipment was supplied and installed by Columbus Heating and Ventilating Co. Heat was supplied to the auditorium by three hot-air furnaces and three suction fans, while a separate steam heat system supplied heat to the stage, offices and tenant spaces. A large ventilation fan, capable of moving up to forty-four thousand cubic feet of air per minute, was located in the basement and supplied the building with ventilation through a huge shaft on the roof. The air was directed over the furnaces in the winter and supplied cool air (or at least cooler air) in the summer. Also in the summer, two rooftop fans supplied additional ventilation. Exhaust air left the building through vents on both sides of the theatre.[228]

Measuring forty-nine by twenty-eight feet, the proscenium stage was designed to accommodate the largest of traveling shows at the time. The stage provided an acting area of thirty-eight by twenty-eight feet. With these

Opposite, top: On March 16, 1928, steel was being erected throughout the retail, auditorium and stage areas. *Courtesy of the Marion County Historical Society.*

Opposite, bottom: On April 2, 1928, steel work continued upward for the second and third floors and the auditorium. *Courtesy of the Palace Cultural Arts Association.*

BUILDING A PALACE

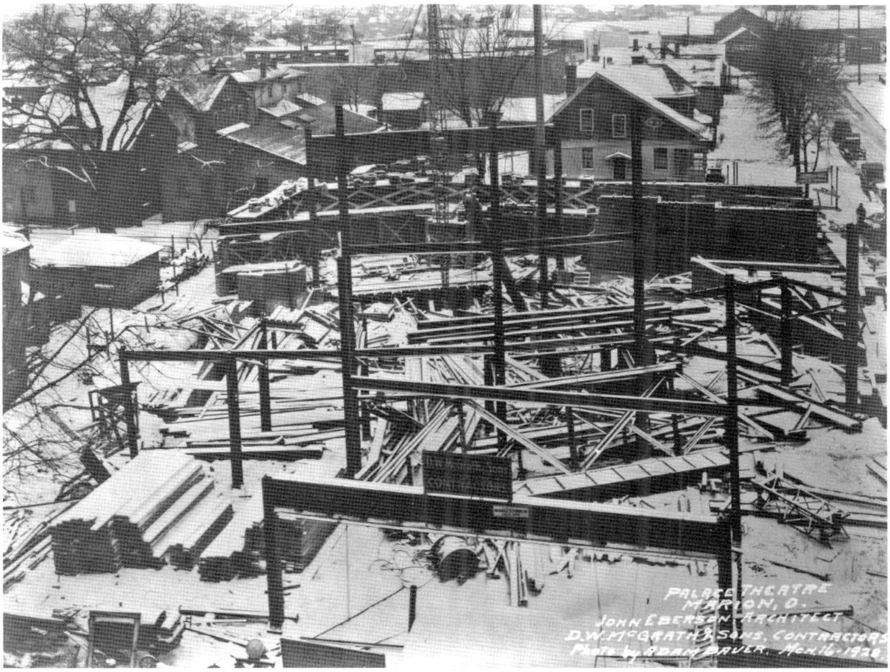

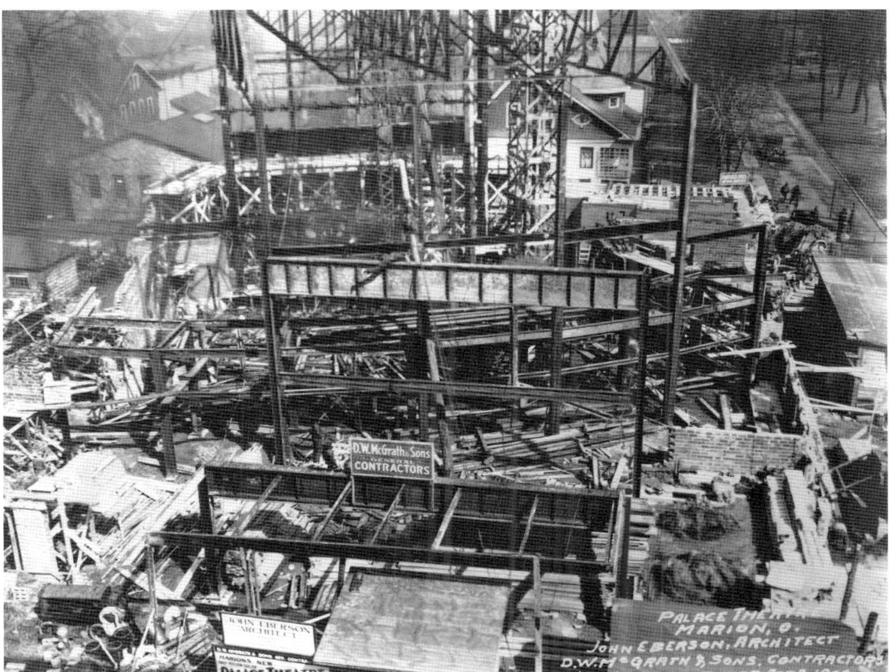

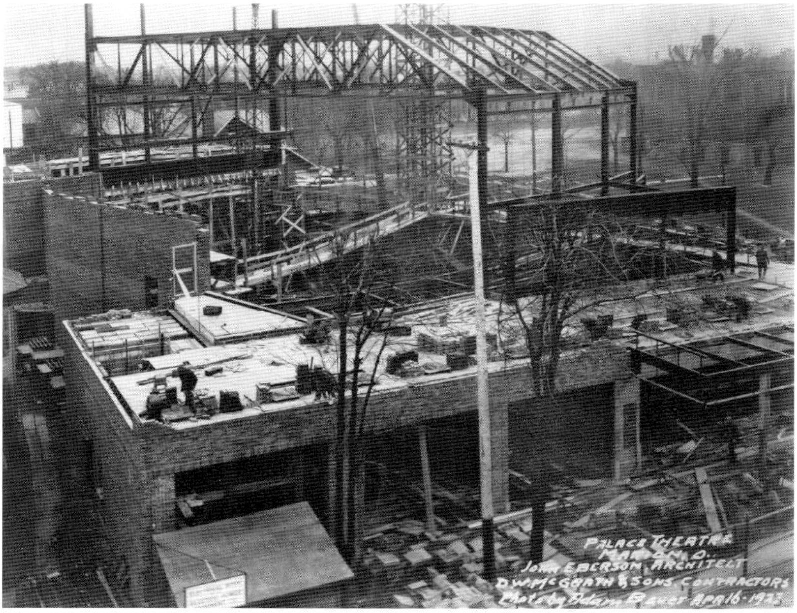

By April 16, 1928, brick workers had made good progress. *Courtesy of the Marion County Historical Society.*

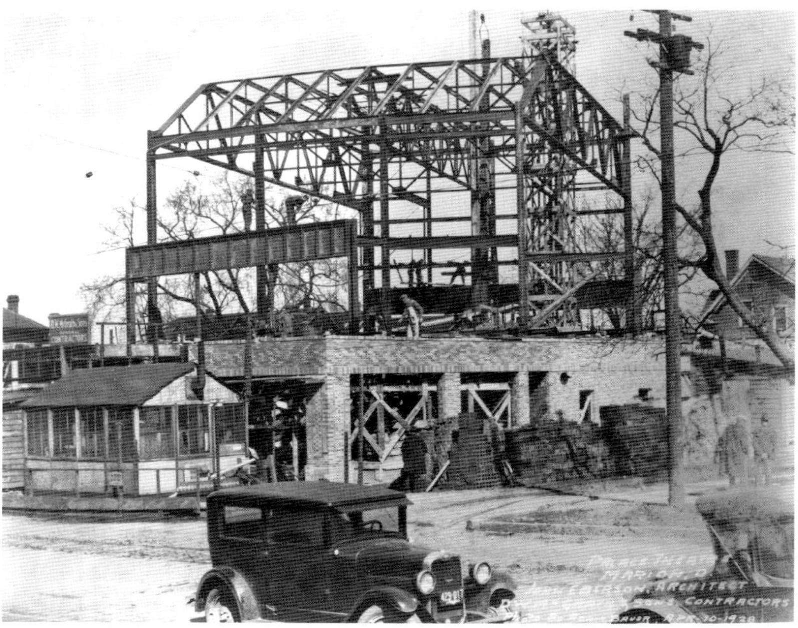

Brick and steel work continued on April 30, 1928. *Courtesy of the Marion County Historical Society.*

dimensions, the Palace stage size and acting area were comparable to the largest Broadway theatres.

Lighting was controlled from three switching areas, one at stage right (the audience's left), one in the projection room and one in a room off the lobby.[229] These controlled the atmospheric lighting around the theatre, the lighting in the front of the building and outside and all lights on stage, including the footlights (now removed) and border lights. In front of the balcony, six large spotlights were permanently installed.[230]

The building façades, embellishments, cornices and other decorative ornaments inside the theatre were formed from plaster. First, rubber molds were made to produce the ornamentation for walls.[231] The individual pieces were made by pouring wet plaster into the mold. Once dry, the mold was removed, and any finishing work on the piece was completed. Next, the piece was lettered and numbered to aid in construction, packed and shipped to the theatre site, usually by rail. Once at the site, the unpainted plaster pieces were uncrated on the theatre auditorium floor and organized for

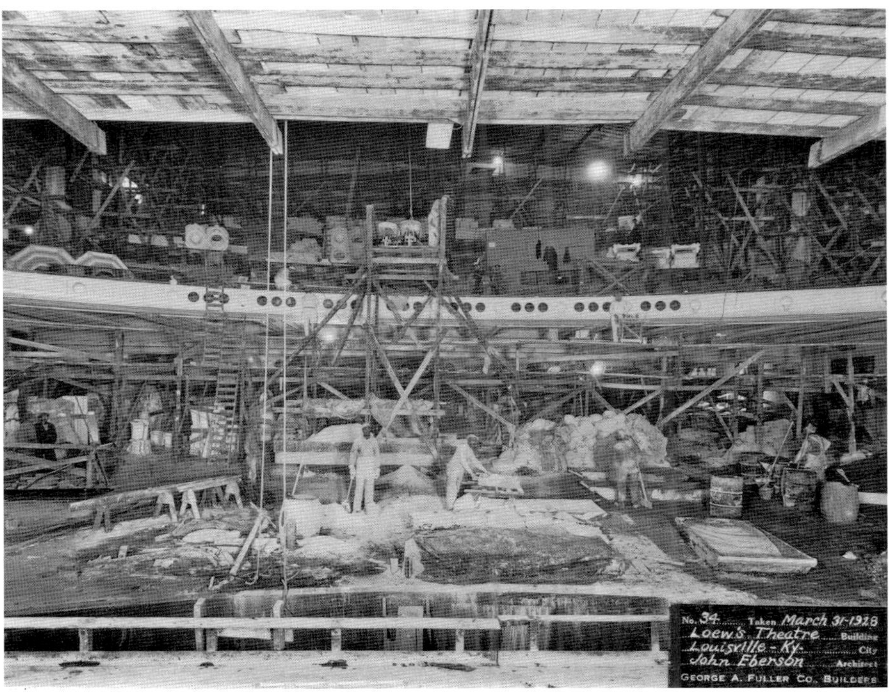

Plasterwork underway at the Louisville Palace Theatre. Similar construction techniques were used at the Marion Palace. In the left rear are premade decorations and vases that were shipped to the site. *Courtesy of the Library of Congress.*

assembly. Without the care of labeling, assembly would have taken more time—an almost impossible jigsaw puzzle. But it was far from a puzzle; each piece was carefully planned for a precise location and identified on drawings.

Eberson reused design molds, varying which molds were used from theatre to theatre. By doing so, he kept costs low yet made each theatre design unique. Ornamental plaster designs found at the Marion Palace were used in slightly different ways in other theatres, but the complete design was not repeated elsewhere.

Various methods were used to install the plaster pieces in the theatres. For a niche, for example, a section of plaster wall was left open to receive the preformed piece, which was affixed with screws to support wood. For

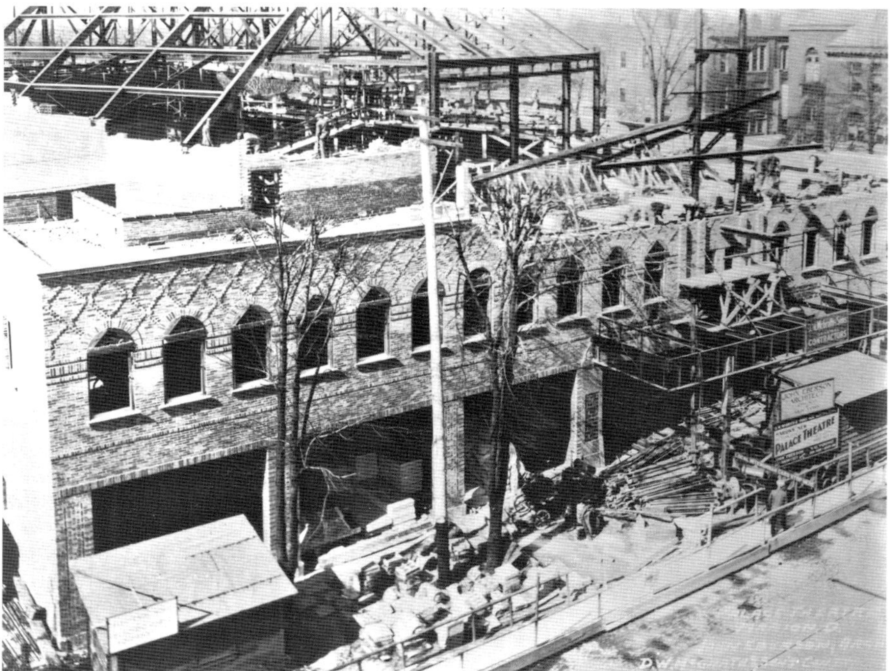

Second-floor brickwork was completed by May 6, 1928. *Courtesy of the Marion County Historical Society.*

Opposite, top: Exterior brickwork was completed by May 16, 1928, except for the tower. A large fan and air handling system parts had arrived for installation. *Courtesy of the Palace Cultural Arts Association.*

Opposite, bottom: The brickwork was complete by June 8, 1928. The two steel beams would hold the vertical sign. *Courtesy of the Palace Cultural Arts Association.*

BUILDING A PALACE

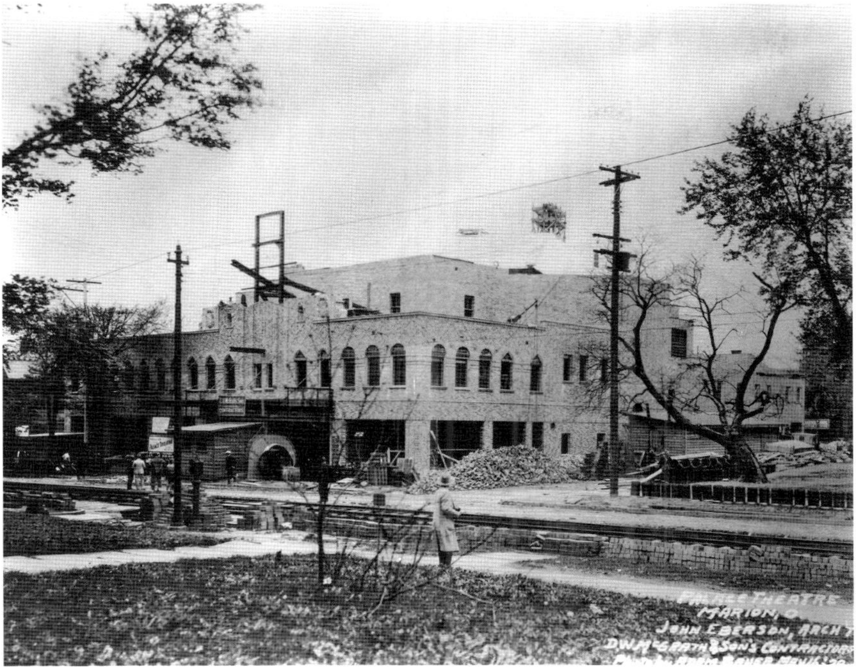

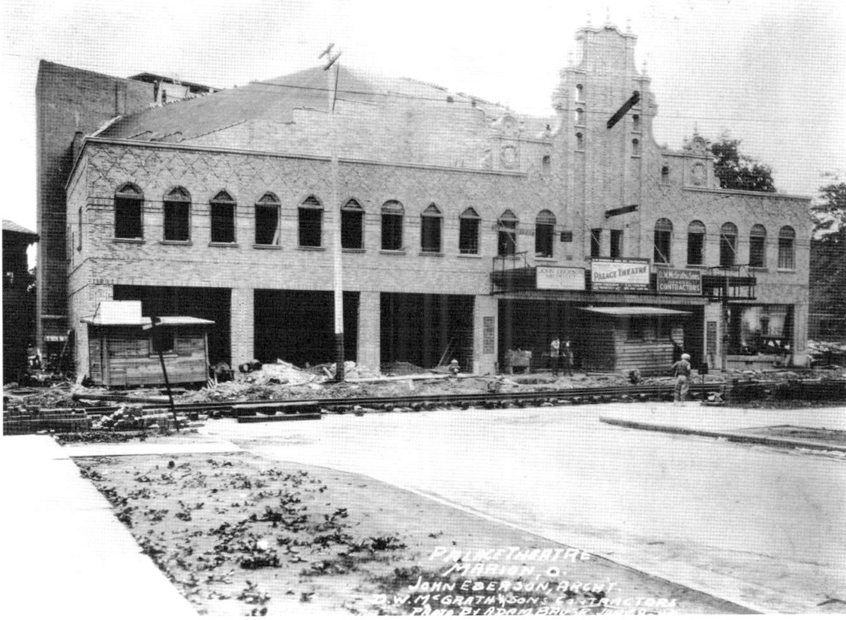

the towers and balconies, wood frames were constructed, and large plaster pieces were then attached to the wood frame, again with screws. Plaster was then applied to fill any seams and holes.

The finishing work was completed by employees of Eberson's Michael Angelo Studios. The company employed a total of about thirty people, although not all employees worked on every theatre. When several of these employees arrived in Marion, it was their job to install the plaster ornamentation; place the statues, trees and birds; and paint the interior.[232] The Eberson family was actively involved in all theatre installations. Eberson's wife and daughter made the banners used in the theatres, and Drew Eberson or his mother ordered and placed the statuary, and Drew mapped out the locations of the stars on the ceilings.[233]

Other contractors and suppliers for the Palace were Wyandot Clay Products Co.; Upper Sandusky, Ohio (bricks); Marion Sand & Gravel Co., Marion (sand); T.M. Cunningham (plumbing and steam piping); Electric Power Equipment Co., Columbus (electric); Ardit Mosaic Tile & Marble Co., Columbus (tile and terrazzo); C.W. Olson Manufacturing Co., Minneapolis (ornamental iron and bronze work); and Millard Hunt Co., Marion (fireproof building materials).

Construction of the "Half Million Dollar Palace" ($6,850,000 in 2014 dollars) took just eight months after excavation work was completed. Construction began on January 1, 1928. The theatre opened on August 30, 1928.

6

A MUSEUM ON THE WALLS

Pietro Caproni's Statues

The illusion of a courtyard setting is further enhanced by the beautiful statues that are strategically placed throughout the Palace. Almost all of these are originals produced by Pietro Paulo Caproni (1862–1928) and his firm, P.P. Caproni and Brother.

With his brother, Emilio, the Caproni firm supplied plaster cast sculptures identical to the Palace casts to schools, museums and theatres throughout America, including Symphony Hall in Boston. Eberson used them in all of his atmospheric theatres. Caproni believed that "the quality of a reproduction is of the greatest importance. In an original work of merit there is a subtleness of treatment—a certain feeling which, if captured in reproduction, places the finished piece within the realm of art itself."

Caproni, originally from Florence, Italy, created a career and business from producing quality reproductions of pieces of art. During the 1880s and 1890s, he traveled throughout Europe making molds directly from masterpieces in museums such as the Louvre, the National Museum in Athens, the Vatican, the Uffizi Gallery in Florence and the British Museum. Because he had the reputation in the art world of being a master craftsman, Caproni was permitted to prepare cast molds directly from museum pieces. This access, coupled with his casting techniques, resulted in reproductions that have highly detailed features not found in most plaster reproductions.

P.P. Caproni and Brother began business in Boston in 1892, where manufacturing and sales operations were based until the business was sold in 1927. Caproni died in 1928. At the height of production, 2,500 different plaster casts were available for sale, including the full-sized *Winged Victory of Samothrace* and Michelangelo's head of *David*. Today, some of Caproni's original molds survive and are used by the Giust Gallery in Boston.

After 1927, the company was bought and sold many times, usually because of a lack of customers with interest in copied artwork. Yet the quality of the original molds and techniques had value and were sold to successive owners. After the original buildings were converted to residential condominiums, castings continued at a gallery in Woburn, Massachusetts. The owner, Robert Shure, a plaster cast and bronze expert, has recovered many more original vintage Caproni casts to enlarge the collection. The company continues to produce and sell many Caproni casts.

Copies of the Caproni catalogue are still available at libraries. The availability of these catalogues, coupled with research on some of the actual statues, tells us with certainty that, except for two pieces (and perhaps four), the Palace statues are from the Caproni studios. Part of the evidence comes from the catalogues and part from the observation of the details of the reproductions and approximate measurements taken of the plaster casts. Further proof is found in the base of each cast;

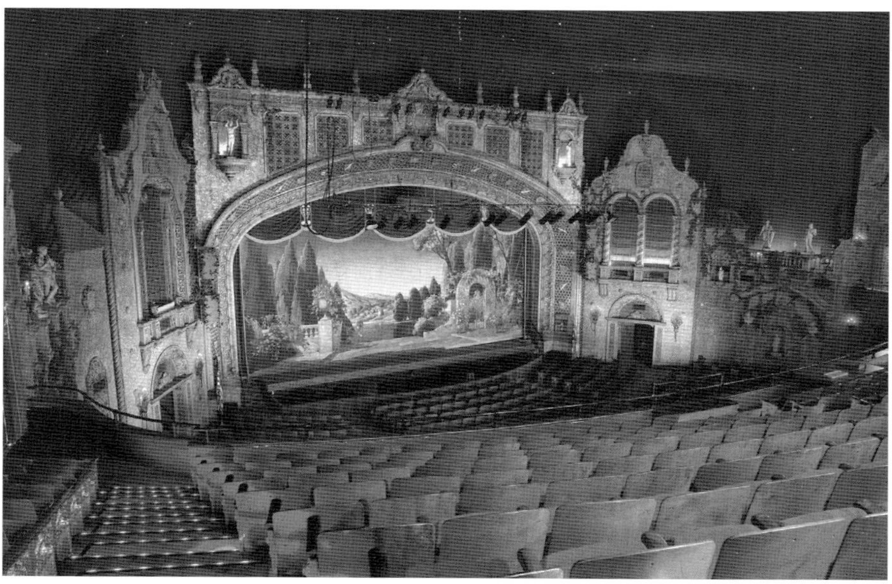

The interior of the Marion Palace Theatre. A view of the stage from the balcony, circa 1990. The original fire curtain, shown here, is infrequently displayed. Stars are simulated for the photo. *Courtesy of the Palace Cultural Arts Association.*

Caproni embedded a metal (brass and, later, aluminum), oval-shaped hallmark in the bottom of his work, embossed with "P.P. Caproni & Bro., Boston, Mass." With the exception of one photograph of a section of the east wall, records are unavailable to determine the original placement of the statues.

While it cannot be confirmed, it is likely that the Palace statues were purchased by Eberson's wife, Beatrice, in connection with her role as director of Michael Angelo Studios. This would have allowed the Ebersons to purchase the casts directly and then add a fee to the overall cost to compensate the studio for its design work. This total cost was then charged to Young Amusement Company. The practice was common in the 1920s and provided John Eberson with more control over (and compensation for) the interior design that was so integral to an atmospheric theatre. At the time, Michael Angelo Studios was located in Chicago. It later moved to New York City, in connection with the move there by the Eberson family. A congratulatory advertisement appeared in the *Marion Star* by Michael Angelo Studios on August 29, 1928. The ad noted that the interior decorating was done by the studio.

The Praying Boy

Proscenium, Upper Left

(School of Greek sculptor Lysipp, 300 BCE, National Museum, Berlin. Bronze.)

One of the most famous ancient sculptures, *The Praying Boy* was rediscovered on the Island of Rhoades. From that time, it has been traced to Venice, the court of Louis XIV and the court of Frederick the Great. It was abducted to Paris by Napoleon in 1807 and returned to Germany in 1830. The arms of the statue were added at a later date, with the effect that it appears to be a praying boy. It is thought that originally the boy was holding some sacrificial vessel. Eberson's placement of the statue was likely intentional. This subtle reference to God further added to the illusion that theatre patrons were outside and looking up at a star-filled heaven.

Capitoline Antinous

Proscenium, Upper Right

(Roman copy of Greek statue, Capitoline Museum, Rome. Marble.)

The *Capitoline Antinous* was discovered in the ruins of Hadrian's villa in Tivoli. It was regarded as one of the most beautiful Roman copies of a Greek statue then found. Originally thought to be a sculpture of Hadrian's favorite male lover, Antinous, it is now generally regarded as a sculpture representing Hermes, the Greek god of shepherds, travelers, merchants and thieves. Yet the athletic body is of the type that is consistent with Antinous types and may mean that the head was added at a later date.

Unidentified Statue
West Wall, Orchestra, Above Organ Grille
The small statue above the organ grille has neither been inspected nor identified. It does not appear in the Caproni catalogue, although the company did not list every piece that was available for sale.

Diana (Artemis) de Gabies (Diana Robing)
West Wall, Upper Balcony
(Roman copy of Greek original attributed to Praxiteles, 400 BCE, Louvre. Marble.)
This sculpture was discovered in 1792 by Gavin Hamilton at Gabii, Italy. It was owned by the Borghese family and later purchased by the Louvre. Artemis was the Greek goddess of hunting and childbirth and protector of young girls until marriage. Diana (Artemis) is the only god or goddess represented twice in the Palace; a bust is located on the east wall.

Aphrodite (Venus de Milo)
West Wall, Upper Balcony, Niche
(Alexandros of Antioch, 130 BCE, Louvre. Marble.)
Perhaps the most known sculpture from the Ancient World, only the bust of Aphrodite appears at the Palace, in a small round niche on the balcony level. The arms are missing in the original, a detail carried through in this plaster cast. The statue of Aphrodite (Venus), the goddess of love, was discovered in 1820 by a peasant on the Island of Milo in the Aegean and was later purchased for the Louvre. Children may know the sculpture from the Disney movie *Hercules*, in which Hercules accidentally breaks off her arms while skipping a rock.

Satyr Playing on the Lute
West Wall, Orchestra, Middle, Right
(Roman copy of Greek original, first or second century, 300–380 BCE, Louvre. Marble.)
The satyr, half man, half goat, has goat ears in this statue and was once part of the Borghese collection. In Greek mythology, a satyr was a companion of the god Pan. The statue has been incorrectly identified as a representation of Pan and also incorrectly by Caproni as a faun, which is typically represented

with goat horns. Satyrs, children of nature, represent a free and carefree life. Because of their love of wine, they were frequent representations on Greek wine cups.

Nero as a Child in Toga with a Bulla
West Wall, Orchestra, Middle, Left
(Head dates from third century CE, body does not belong to head, Louvre. Marble.)
Nero, emperor of Rome (37–68 CE), is shown as a boy. During his reign, Nero expanded cultural opportunities for Romans, including the construction of new theatres. There was a belief at the time that theatre led to immorality. Undaunted, Nero established the quinquennial Neronia, a festival that included games, poetry and theatre. This plaster cast is catalogued by the Caproni firm as Augustus in youth. While Nero's name included Augustus, the original sculpture is commonly referred to as *Nero in Youth* or *Nero as a Child*.

Gold Bust (Not Original)
West Wall, Orchestra, Under Balcony, Niche
While a small bust has been placed in the niche on the west wall, main floor, under the balcony, it is not original to the Palace. It is much lighter in weight than a Caproni cast, bears no hallmark and has been painted gold.

Doryphoros, After Polykleitos
East Wall, Orchestra, Upper, Right
(Roman copy of Greek original by Polykleitos, 440 BCE, Naples National Archeological Museum. Marble.)
The athletic *Spear-Bearer* (the original statue once held a spear) is considered the most famous work of Greek sculpture. The original bronze was made by Polyclitus as a reference work on the most precise proportions and measurements for a sculpture of the human body. He also wrote a treatise on sculpture in which he recorded these measurements; it has not survived.

Claudius in Youth
East Wall, Orchestra, Upper, Left
(Louvre. Marble.)
Claudius (emperor, 41–54 BCE) rebuilt one of the first permanent theatres in Ancient Rome, the Theatre of Pompey, after it was destroyed by fire. He was the father of Nero, a statue of whom, also in youth, appears on the west wall. Both statues show the men in youth, and both are depicted in almost identical clothing and poses.

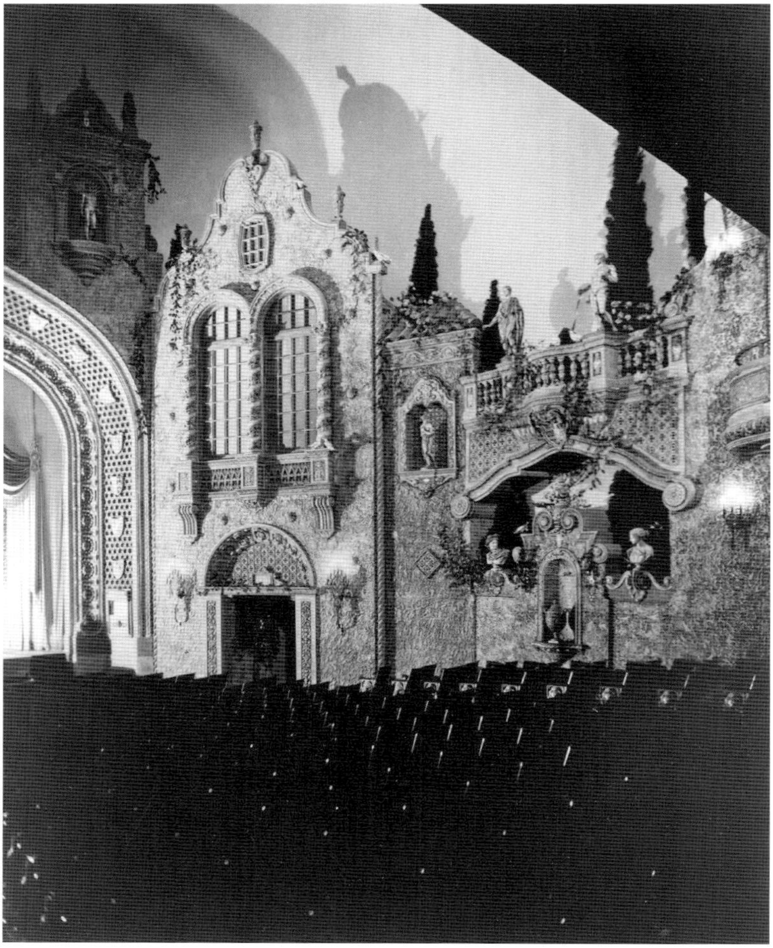

The east wall of the Marion Palace Theatre, circa 1928. Note that a vase was originally placed in the niche where the statue of Hebe now stands. This image also shows where artificial trees were once installed to create the outdoor illusion. *Courtesy of the Theatre Historical Society of America.*

Hebe Bearing Cup (Not Original)
East Wall, Orchestra, Lower, Middle
(Berthel Thorvaldsen, 1806, Thorvaldsens Museum, Copenhagen. Marble)
This statue is not an original installation and has a different finish than the Caproni statues. When the Palace opened, a large vase was set in the niche. Hebe, the goddess of youth, is usually depicted, as here, carrying a cup. She was the goddess who provided the drink of immortality to the other gods

and goddesses. The plaster cast of this statue was unavailable in the early Caproni catalogues. It was offered for sale in the 1920s, however. The maker of this reproduction is not known.

Apollo Belvedere
East Wall, Orchestra, Lower, Left Bust
(Roman copy of Greek original bronze, 120–140 CE, Vatican. Marble.)
The bust of Apollo is from the statue of Apollo in which he is depicted as shooting an arrow. Apollo, son of Zeus, is frequently depicted as youthful and athletic. He was the patron god of light and sun, truth, music and poetry. In modern times, many theatres have been named for him, as the god of music, including the famous Apollo Theatre in Harlem.

Diana (Artemis) of Versailles
East Wall, Orchestra, Lower, Right Bust
(Roman copy of Greek original bronze, first or second century, Versailles. Marble.)
The bust of Artemis (called Diana by the Romans) is from a statue of the goddess, known as a huntress, with a deer. It is installed in the Galerie des Caryatidesin of the Louvre, a special area designed for the statue.

Diana, daughter of Zeus and twin sister of Apollo, was the goddess of the hunt and wild animals. Some historians believe that she may predate the Greeks as a subject of veneration.

Unidentified Statue
East Wall, Orchestra, Small Statue Closest to Stage
Because of the location, the statue is not easily identifiable. Nothing similar is found in the Caproni catalogues. The photographic record reveals that a different statue, also unidentified, was originally installed in this location.

Unidentified Statue
Circular Niche above East Balcony Exit
This niche is now empty. In a circa 1975 photograph, a bust of Aphrodite (Venus de Milo) is placed in this niche. That bust is now located in a niche on the west wall, upper balcony. The original location of the bust is not known.

George Washington
(Loredo Taft, 1909, University of Washington, Seattle. Bronze.)
The statute of Washington was created for the Alaska Yukon Pacific Exhibition held in Seattle in 1909. The fairgrounds became the campus of

the University of Washington, where the statue still stands. Loredo Taft, who created the sculpture, is known to have sought creative help with sculpture techniques from Pietro Caproni, which likely helped the Caproni firm in obtaining a license from Taft to reproduce the work.

The statue portrays an austere Washington in Revolutionary War period clothing, including a long cape, vest and boots. He holds a sheathed sword with his left hand calmly resting over his right hand, which is cupped over the hilt. It is a pose of confidence, tempered by wisdom. The only indication of Washington's military success is a lion's head on the cross guard—a traditional symbol of power and dominance in Ancient Greece, Rome and England.

PART V

OFF THE STAGE

7

THE PALACE OFFICES AND SHOPS

Like other theatre buildings of the period, the Palace was designed to generate revenue from both ticket sales and rental income. Eberson designed the theatre building to maximize street-front retail space. In an age when most people still walked to shop, see professionals and socialize, window advertising was important to a business's success. Except for the lobby doors, theatre exit areas and the stage, almost every other available street-front space at the Palace could be leased.

Consequently, the lobby area is small, although the high ceilings and wide staircase to the balcony create the illusion of more space. The lobby appears larger today because glass doors have been added on the east and west sides, which open to the new concession area and the new box office. A reproduction of the original box office, a tiny cubicle fronting West Center Street, is used for ticket will call and movie ticket sales.

The Harding Hotel and Palace Theatre significantly increased demand for office and retail space along West Center Street. Real estate values also increased as the area became the center for entertainment, society events and lodging. When the Palace opened, the *Marion Star* reported that negotiations were underway to lease a nearby retail site for between \$700 and \$800 (annually) per front foot. A year earlier, the same sites would have been leased for between \$500 and \$600.[234]

The Palace owners wanted only high-quality tenants in the building—tenants who could afford the rent, would not interfere with theatre operations, would not

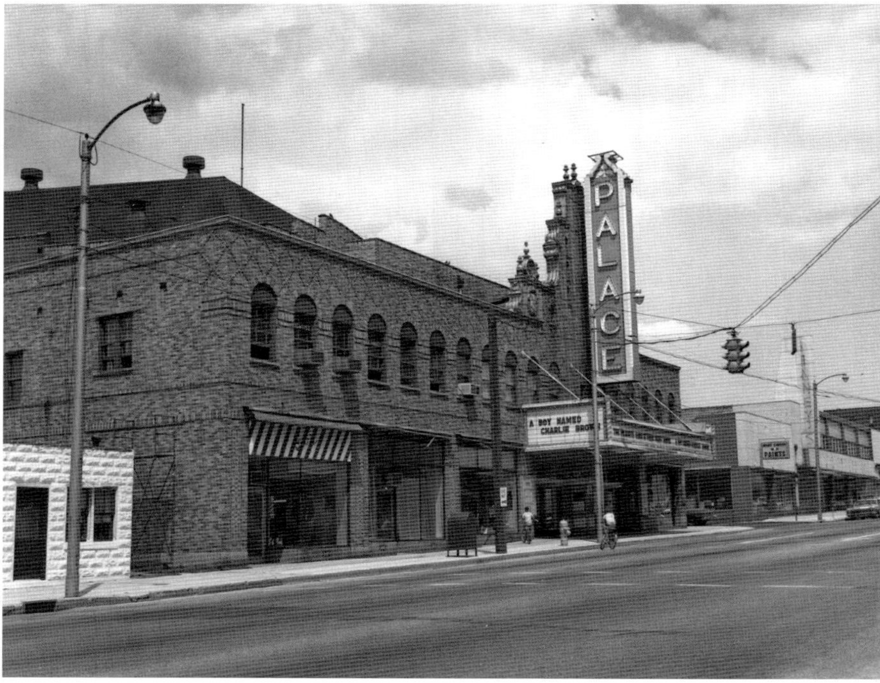

A view of the Palace in 1970. Dr. Finney, a dentist, was located on the second floor. A barbershop rented space on the street level. *Courtesy of the Palace Cultural Arts Association.*

embarrass the owners and would help the theatre gain immediate acceptance in the community. To accomplish these goals, R.T. Lewis, a real estate broker, was retained to lease the space.

In July 1928, the Palace management and a group of doctors and a dentist announced the lease of 80 percent of the second-floor office suites to create "one of the most thorough and complete clinics for the diagnosis and treatment of diseases in the state."[235] These leases guaranteed respectability for the Palace and foot traffic that would not interfere with the Palace's evening performances. The creation of the clinic made the Palace seem to be on the cutting edge. The age of medical specialists had begun at this time, and a clinic was thought to provide excellent medical care.

The clinic members were Dr. Filmore Young, a heart specialist, who leased four front rooms at the west end of the building; Dr. E.W. Imbody, a pharmacy graduate of Ohio Northern University and an oral surgeon, who rented six rooms next to Dr. Young; Dr. A.J. Willey, a thyroid gland surgeon, who leased four rooms next to the Imbody suite; and Dr. E.O. Richardson, an eye, ear, nose and throat specialist, who rented two rooms on the north side facing Campbell Street.[236]

The rental space included more than physician examination rooms. The medical clinic was equipped with a full laboratory and medical diagnosis and testing equipment. This included chemical and clinical laboratories, radium, X-ray with high-voltage deep therapy for malignancy, electro-radiograph and polygraph, ultraviolet and diathermy.[237] The clinic offices opened on September 1, 1928.[238]

There were no elevators that allowed patients to access the second floor. Stairways from street level on the southwest (off West Center Street) and east end (off Campbell Street) of the building provided the only access to the second-floor offices. The second-story location, while difficult for some patients to access, allowed for better air circulation and was a less expensive alternative to higher first-floor rental rates. In a time when few two-story buildings had elevators, patients did not expect anything other than to climb stairs.

The downtown, second-story medical space was typical for many towns and cities at the time. Before physicians moved downtown, most had offices in their homes or in some cases in separate buildings at their homes. New physician office space, like that rented at the Palace, would have been preferred by many patients. A physician's home office was often cluttered and lacked privacy. The examination room, office and waiting room were all the same. Also, standards of the practice of asepsis (the prevention of infection by maintaining sterile conditions) had developed since the early 1920s, and home offices could not provide a high level of cleanliness.

The fifth office suite on the second floor was leased to a beauty parlor, which opened the first week of September 1928.[239] The business was owned by Mr. L.C. Stuckert, who also managed the beauty parlor across the street at the Harding Hotel. The shop was located on the southeast corner of the Palace building, with windows overlooking both West Center and Campbell Streets.[240] The windows and resulting cross-ventilation made the location good for the beauty shop.

The shop operated five booths, which were leased to individual stylists. When the Palace first opened, the woman's bob was in full style, although more feminine styles were returning to favor. The shop would have included at least one permanent machine, which created the curl look that was popular with some women, and several hair dryers. Permanents, including shampoo, were fifteen dollars. A facial treatment cost two dollars. The shop also offered hair thinning treatments, marcels (hair waves made by hot curling tongs), finger waves and manicures. Schoolgirls could get a marcel or finger wave for seventy-five cents.

An apartment was located in the rear of the second-story office suite area, on the west side of the building. It included two rooms and a bath.[241] Whether it was rented by one of the Palace employees is not known, although its proximity to these offices and the beauty shop likely made it less than desirable.

On the first floor, two of the five available spaces had been rented when the theatre opened. The Faultless Dry Cleaners had rented one of the five spaces[242] and the Palace Art and Gift Shop another.[243] Only the gift shop opened at the same time as the theatre.[244] Additional construction to build out the space for the other businesses was still needed.

Mildred Walker and Eta Mae Miller owned the gift shop, which was decorated using red and black colors.[245] It was located in the first-floor space, second from the left of the theatre lobby doors. The shop sold lingerie, toilet articles, pocketbooks, compacts, bridge scores and tallies, paintings and

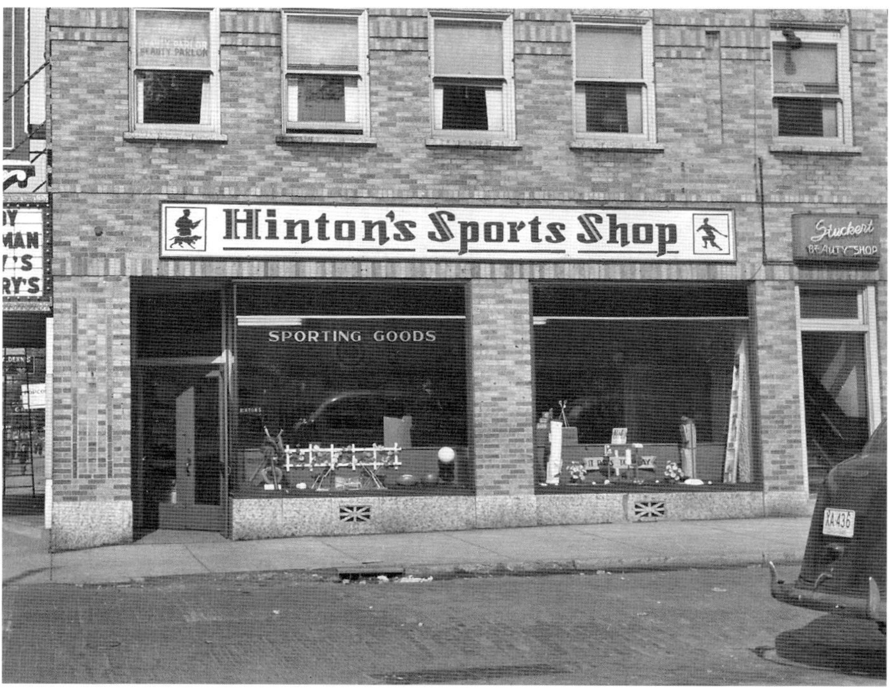

The Palace, circa 1950s. Hinton's Sporting Goods occupied the corner retail space. Stuckert's Beauty Shop was on the second floor. Just beyond the marquee is a sign for W.A. Dennis, optician. *Courtesy of the Palace Cultural Arts Association.*

novelties, which the women purchased in Chicago on buying trips.[246] Both women also taught painting and art classes at the store.[247]

Faultless Dry Cleaners opened its second finishing and pick-up location at the Palace. The other was on East Church Street, and its plant was on Farming Street. It advertised one-day service if clothes were dropped off by 8:00 a.m. The location at the Palace ensured a steady stream of orders from the acts that played at the theatre.

In December 1928, Jess T. Dowler & Son, a radio store, opened at the Palace. The owners had been in the radio business for four years, operating out of Jess Dowler's home on Windsor Street, a few blocks to the south of the Palace. The store featured Sonora radios, which were manufactured in Chicago.

Also opened in 1928 was Jackson's Cut-Rate, the first store at the Palace to sell food. It had a soda fountain and sold sandwiches, light lunches, candy and homemade pastries. A second location was at 140 South Main Street. The store also sold greeting cards, toiletries, cigars and a variety of convenience items, such as razor blades and toothpaste.

On the Campbell Street side, R.A. Harrison opened a small silk hosiery shop, where he also made repairs to hosiery with tears and holes. It isn't clear when the store was opened, but it was sometime in late 1928 or early 1929.

After these initial offices and stores closed, new tenants replaced them. Some of these are listed in the accompanying table. Today, all of the rental space has been redesigned for use in Palace operations. The space once occupied by Dr. Richardson and Stuckert's Beauty Shoppe is now office space. The rest of the second-floor space is used for additional Palace offices, a small kitchen and a multipurpose room (the Scharer Patron Lounge). The former residential apartment is also part of that space. Stairs that once led to the second-floor space on the west end have been closed. Doors now connect the old space to the second floor of the Palace Pavilion event space.

On the street level, the retail rental space has been repurposed as well. The west side of the first floor is now a concession room (the Marion Rotary Room) and is also used as a multipurpose room. The east side is used as a box office and reception area. An additional rental space facing Campbell Street is used for storage.

Table 2
PALACE RETAIL TENANTS

Adding Machine & Typewriter Exchange (1935)
Contoure Shop, the (1935)
Delux Dry Cleaners (1937)
Dennis, W.A., OD (1950s), optometrist
Dunbar, Marion A., Dr. (1957), dentist
R.E. Eicher (1975)
Elsey's Modern Appliances (1950s)
Famous Brand Shoes (1962)
Faultless Dry Cleaners
Finney, H. Ray, Dr. (1959)
Florsheim Shoes (1960s)
Gift Center, the (1940s)
Havana Salon of Beauty (1947)
Hinton's Sports Shop (1940s, 1950s)
Imbody, E.W., Dr.
Jackson's Cut-Rate (1928)
Jess T. Dowler & Son (1928), radios
Kirby Cleaner Co. (1946)
Linda Lou Dress Shop (1945), women's clothing
Nelson Realty (1956)
Odell Thompson Loan & Finance Co.
Palace Art & Gift Shop (1928)
Palace Gift Shop (1950s)
Patrick Realty (1962)
Pugh Brothers Jewelers (1953)
R.A. Harrison Shoppe (1929), shoes; silk hose repair
Richardson, E.O., Dr.
Shealty Equipment Co. (1940)
Smith, Clare W., MD (1950s)
Stuckert's Beauty Shop
Stull & Fields Appliances (1950s)
Westheimer & Co. (1959), stockbroker
Wick's Shoe Store (1960s)
Willey, A.J., Dr.
Young, Filmore, Dr.

**original tenants in bold*

8

MUSIC AT THE PALACE

The Organ and the Orchestra

Theatres built around the time of the Palace were expected to have an organ. It provided music during intermissions and gave life to silent motion pictures, conveying setting, mood and character. After the last performance, the organist's chase music, usually a march, let the audience know it was time to leave the theatre.

The organist and the organ itself were considered stars, equal to those on the screen and on the stage. The organist could reproduce train whistles, Chinese gongs, castanets, tambourines, tom-toms, steamboat whistles, sirens, fire gongs, telephones, claxons, sleigh bells and chirping birds. In addition to sound effects, the organ could be played to sound like a marimba, harp, piano, glockenspiel, xylophone, snare and bass drums, cymbals, triangle and wood block.

The original organ for the Marion Palace was not the 3/10 Mighty Wurlitzer Theatre Pipe Organ installed in 1976. Instead, it was an ornate, three-manual Page Rainbo Gold, made specifically for the Palace. The name is from the finish on the organ, which when hit with a spotlight reflected light throughout the theatre.[248] It was also referred to as a Marvel Page Organ.[249] The day after the opening, the *Marion Star* enthused, "Reflecting every color of the rainbow as brilliant hued 'spots' play over its surface, the three-manual Page organ of the Palace theater is a thing of beauty in appearance as well as tone lending in no small way to the artistic effect of the interior."[250]

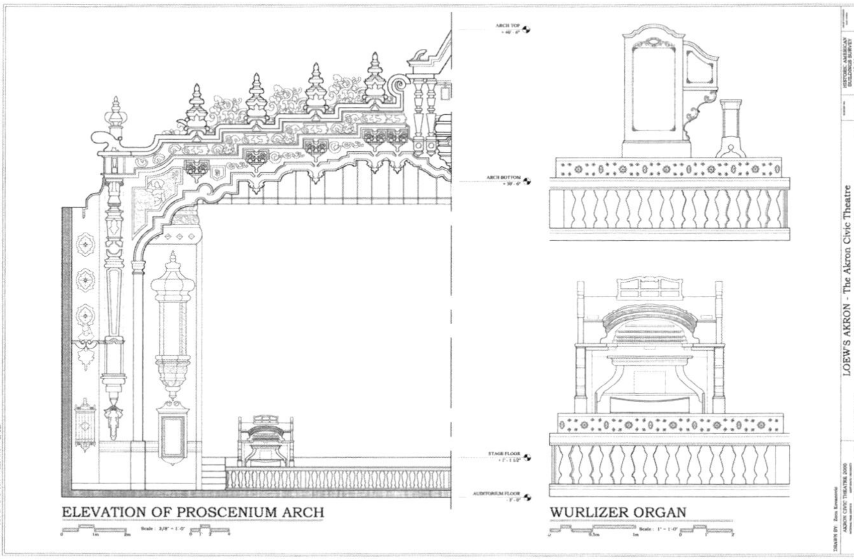

Eberson took great care in designing all parts of the theatre. This is the design for the proscenium and organ platform at the Akron Palace. *Courtesy of the Library of Congress.*

The *Star* further described the organ to its readers:

> *Organs of exquisite tone and ornate appearance have become one of the outstanding features of motion picture houses and the management of Marion's new playhouse invested a huge sum in obtaining one of the best on the market.*
>
> *The organ is custom made being designed especially for the Marion theater. The size of the building and its acoustic properties were taken into consideration before any work was done on the musical instrument.*
>
> *Every bit of material going into the construction of the organ was carefully selected coming from many lands. Many weeks of work were necessary before the instrument was completed and ready to install.*
>
> *The heart of the organ rests in the switchboard. Keys operate silver and bronze contacts making instantaneous connections with the pipes and other effects. The pipes are cleverly concealed on each side of the stage, the opening forming double windows leading to balconies of two Spanish towers. The chambers form a natural part of the architecture of the interior.*
>
> *The console is the only part of the huge organ visible. It rests on a platform that can be raised and lowered bringing the console up to a*

> *point where it can be viewed to a great advantage all over the house or lowered to a point where it does not interfere with the view of the stage. The elevator is controlled by a motor located in a soundproof room back of the stage.*
>
> *The console itself is known as the Page Rainbo Gold deriving its name from the finish. It is heavily scrolled and so finished that lights are reflected in a very effective fashion.*[251]

The *Star*'s interest in the organ was not one of mere technological curiosity. The theatre organ was as much a part of the Palace as the marquee outside or the clouds drifting overhead.

The Page Organ Company, which made the organ, was a producer of theatre pipe organs, located in Lima, Ohio. The company started with a home-built organ in 1922, expanding as the demand for theatre organs increased. With the introduction of talkies and the elimination of new theatre construction during the Great Depression, the demand for organs declined and with it the company's solvency. The assets were sold in 1930 to Ellsworth Beilharz, an employee. He owned the company until 1984, when it was sold to two employees, who remain in business under the name Lima Pipe Organ Company, Inc.

Page organs are still in operation and can be found at Catalina Casino, Avalon, California; Embassy Theatre, Fort Wayne, Indiana; Paramount Theatre, Anderson, Indiana; the Hedback Community Theatre in Indianapolis (Page/Wurlitzer organ); and Stephenson High School in DeKalb County, Georgia.

The Page organs at the Paramount Theatre (1929) in Anderson, Indiana, and Emboyd (Embassy) Theatre (1928) in Fort Wayne, Indiana, are both in working condition and still at their original installations. Both theatres were designed by John Eberson. It is very likely that these organs were identical or very similar in exterior finish to the one installed at the Marion Palace.

The theatre organist needed to be adept at three skills: the ability to project an energetic stage presence, excellent organ skills and dynamic choir direction. The organist began performing at the matinee, accompanying the first showing of the motion picture. Before the next showing, the organist would lead a community sing, while the words were projected on the theatre screen. These were made entertaining as the organist directed the balcony audience to compete in singing with the main-floor audience or the men against the women. If a vaudeville act was on the bill, the organist would provide sound effects or background music. At intermissions, grand music would be played until the organ disappeared to the bottom of the pit signaling to the audience that the show would soon begin. Each day started early and ended late.[252]

Banks Kennedy, born in Tuscaloosa, Alabama, was the first organist at the Marion Palace. His repertoire included modern and classical music. He also wrote his own compositions. Recognized as a skillful performer, he performed on Chicago radio station KYW, which could be heard in Marion. Kennedy began playing the piano as a child and became interested in the organ while attending the University of Chicago. He had a feature organist position at the Capital Theatre in Chicago.[253] Prior to coming to Marion, Banks played at the Palace Theatre in nearby Canton, Ohio. Because of his success there, the owner of the Marion Palace asked him to come to open the Marion Palace as the guest organist.[254]

As a way to attract audiences to the Marion Palace, he started the Banks Kennedy Kiddie Kindness Klub. On Saturday, September 28, 1928, children were invited to the theatre at 10:00 a.m. for organization of the club, with no admission charge for the first meeting. Club meetings were held every Saturday, when children watched pictures, played games, won prizes and participated in sing-alongs.[255] Banks Kennedy was proclaimed "King of the Kids."

Empty seats were financial losses for a theatre, and every effort was made to keep them filled, especially on Saturday mornings, when adults were busy with errands. For children, the Marion Palace became a destination, inside and out. On October 6, 1928, there was a live appearance by Leo the Lion, the Metro-Goldwyn-Mayer (MGM) trademarked mascot, outside the theatre.[256] The lion traveled to Marion in a $100,000 caravan that included a calliope.[257] Leo also appeared at the children's home.[258]

Kennedy did not stay long in Marion because of the demand for his talent. His tenure at the Palace was never intended to be a long one, and his appearances ended in November 1928. Leo Kindig took his place.[259] He was followed by a number of organists, including Billy Warner,[260] Regal Spencer[261] and Edna Bern.[262]

After leaving Marion, Kennedy returned to his permanent home in New York City, where he had lived since 1924. Contrary to local lore, he was not shot and killed in the 1930s by a mafia boss at the Canton Palace. He died on November 2, 1944, in New York.[263]

In addition to the theatre organ, the Palace opened with its own orchestra, under the direction of Professor Elmer Newstrom. While the organist was the workhorse of the Palace, the audience expected an orchestra for live stage presentations and feature performances. In a 1928 advertisement, the Palace assured the audiences that Newstrom would exceed their expectations:

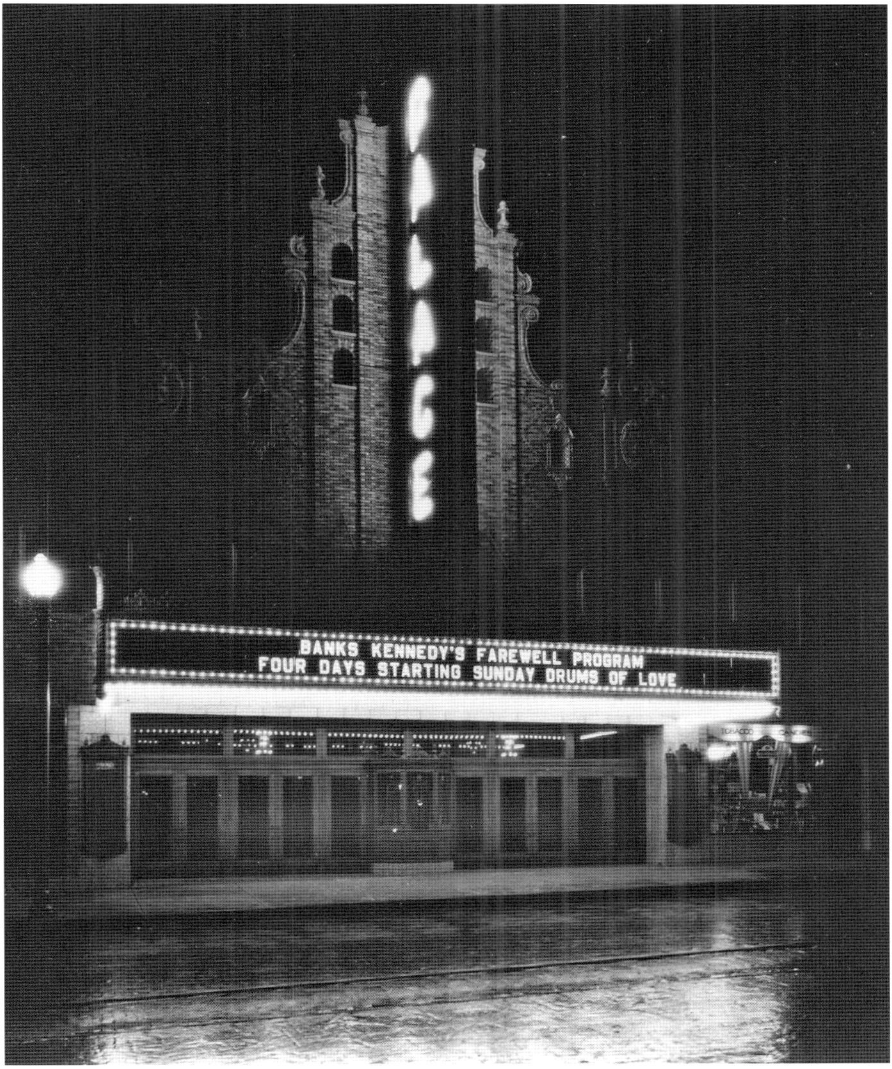

A nighttime photograph of the Palace, November 1928. The marquee announced the final performances of Palace organist Banks Kennedy. *Courtesy of the Marion County Historical Society.*

"Professor Elmer Newstrom, director of the Palace Orchestra, student of the celebrated Harry Diamond, is a recognized leader and director of orchestras. He has been associated with leading theatres of the Chicago district."[264] In addition to conducting the orchestra, he also played the violin and often performed violin solos during theatre programs.

The size of the orchestra was limited by the Palace's operating budget and the size of the orchestra pit. It was designed to be small so that more patron seats could be installed. Some of the pit was actually under the stage, as it remains today. The original orchestra had seven musicians, selected by Newstrom. Just before the opening, efforts were underway to organize the orchestra from the Marion area. The seven instruments included were the piano, violin, trumpet, trombone, flute, clarinet and drums.[265]

Newstrom left Marion in March 1929 after being jailed for his involvement with two sixteen-year-old girls at a late night "illicit party" in February.[266] An "illicit" party was the term used to mean that alcohol, illegal during Prohibition, had been found. He and a companion had taken the girls to a West Center Street hotel room at about 2:00 a.m. and they didn't emerge again until noon the following day. He was sentenced to thirty days in jail and a $200 fine.[267] After his jail term was served, Newstrom relocated to Indiana, where he directed the WIND radio orchestra in the 1930s.

9

POPCORN PALACE

Ask Marionites what they love most about the Palace, and popcorn will be at the top of the list. It wasn't a Popcorn Palace at the beginning. When opened, no drinking or eating was permitted in the theatre. Eating popcorn and other snacks would damage the carpet, not to mention add labor costs to clean up the spilled snacks in between performances. Also, theatres had no room or lobby space designed to make and sell concessions. Theatres lacked a ventilation system for the smoke produced from popping corn and had no adjacent running water for hygiene. To eat in a theatre was considered not only disruptive but also socially unacceptable. Chomping snacks was a behavior associated with the nickelodeon or burlesque house, not a theatre. Also, it was difficult to read movie subtitles while glancing down to eat a snack.

In Marion, businesses competed for thirsty and hungry Palace patrons. Two nearby stores advertised for theatergoer business. Rexall Drugstore, located at the Harding Hotel, advertised in the *Marion Star* the day before opening night, inviting patrons to enjoy "drinks—like you want them" at its soda fountain.[268] Tender's Candyland, owned by Andrew Loukes, advertised candy, ice cream, drinks and sandwiches.[269] It was located one block away, at Center and Oak Streets. A few weeks after the opening, Jackson's Cut-Rate began business in a Palace storefront, selling sandwiches and candy and serving drinks and ice cream from its soda fountain.

All the opposition, justifications and excuses against selling food inside theatres ended with the start of the Great Depression. As theatre owners grew desperate for revenue, they began to realize that concessions were a potentially fat stream of additional income. It isn't known exactly when food sales began in the Palace lobby. If it was like other theatres, however, it began sometime in the mid-1930s.

The profits of popcorn were irresistible. At the time, a ten-pound bag of popcorn kernels sold for twenty-five cents in Marion, at Lawrence Apple Orchards. One bag produced one hundred bags of popcorn, or ten dollars in retail sales. At ten cents a bag, patrons, though hard pressed for cash, could still afford the luxury of a popcorn snack. In fact, unlike candy, popcorn sales actually increased during the Great Depression.

It is possible that the Palace management contracted with another business to sell concessions and allowed the food into the theatre. Other theatres that did this soon changed their minds when it became clear that the patrons' money left the theatre, but the mess stayed in the theatre.

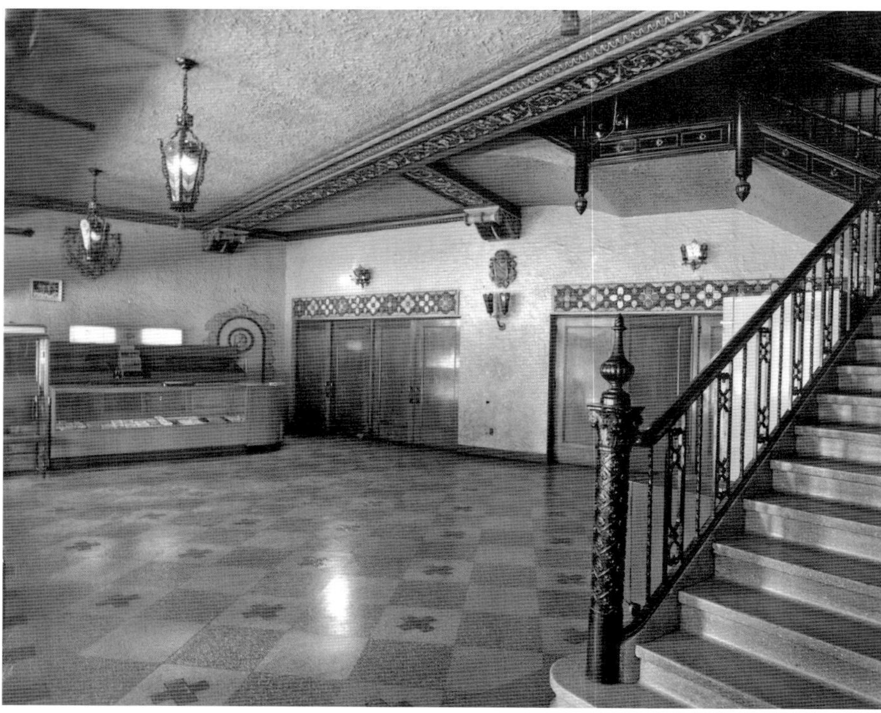

The Palace lobby concession area, 1975. In the 1940s and 1950s, concessions were sold on the opposite side of the lobby. *Courtesy of the Palace Cultural Arts Association. Dale E. Hughes, Inc. Photography.*

At the start of World War II, popcorn sales increased at theatres. Candy was in short supply due to rationing, and popcorn was considered a patriotic snack. It was neither rationed nor imported. Also, Americans were back to work after the Great Depression and had money to spend on movies and popcorn. By 1945, over half of all popcorn sales took place in movie theatres.[270]

After the war, popcorn sales continued to be a major source of theatre revenue. The tie between movies and concession sales was studied closely. Popcorn producers kept track of which movie stars sold the most popcorn (Elvis Presley won in 1958; Bob Hope was second).[271] Theatre owners observed that more popcorn was sold during movies made for children and that popcorn sales were weak during horror shows. Intermissions were added to movies so that patrons had time to buy more popcorn.[272] Short advertisements like "Let's All Go to the Lobby" (1957) were played in the middle of movies. The industry knew one thing quite well: to be profitable, the public needed to keep crunching.

And then came television. Movie attendance plunged from ninety million a week in 1950 to forty million in 1960. Movie theatres began to consolidate and close. Popcorn sales at theatres plummeted but increased for consumption at home.

Today, most exhibitors make the majority of their income at the concession stand because most film distributors demand over 90 percent of the money generated from first-run ticket sales and 50 percent from second-run sales. When movies are shown at the Palace, profitability depends almost exclusively on concession sales, even though the theatre is primarily staffed by volunteers.

10

POLICE RAID AT THE PALACE

Marion has always considered the Palace its prized landmark and center of cultural life. Not the county courthouse, the Warren G. Harding Home, the local Ohio State University campus or even the city's Main Street ever gained that distinction. How a chief of police and a city solicitor concluded that it was a good idea to storm the Palace one hot August night appears as amusingly ill conceived now as it appeared to Marionites then.

At 9:30 p.m. on August 18, 1937, Chief William Marks and a squad of eight policemen rushed through the doors and up to the stage as over one thousand movie patrons watched in disbelief.[273] The police then stopped a sweepstakes that was underway, just after the winner had been announced. The ridiculousness of the raid must have become clear to Marks and city solicitor Ralph Carhart upon hearing boos, jeers and jibes from the audience as the police walked back up the Palace aisles with their booty of sinful sweepstakes devices.[274] They arrested George Planck, the theatre manager, and three box office employees. To make matters worse, the police paraded this dangerous quartet-in-crime, including nineteen-year-old Mary Alice Watts, across the street to police headquarters for booking.[275]

After calming the audience, the remaining Palace employees started the movie. When the Palace closed, the crowd lingered outside in front of the theatre and around the police station. Some tried to peek through the blinds covering the police station windows. Meanwhile, Planck and his employees sat in chairs, freshly booked and processed, waiting for the police to finish their search of evidence. Unhappy with what they had found, the police took Planck back to the Palace to gather more evidence.[276]

The following day, the Palace raid was front-page news: "POLICE ARREST 4 IN RAID ON THEATER SWEEPSTAKES—SQUAD OF 9 HALTS OPERATIONS AT PALACE."[277] Throughout the city, readers' eyes surely rolled in disapproval.

It was, at best, an effort to show that the chief was tough on gambling. The previous December, he'd had his men spread the word that all forms of gambling should cease.[278] At a time when numbers games and other types of gambling were widespread in Marion, the raid on the Palace made little sense, except for political gain. The prosecution of the Palace management was, Carhart crowed in a newspaper interview, believed to be the first of its kind in Ohio—a test case on the legality of movie sweepstakes.[279] Surely statewide headlines and voter attention would follow.

Mayor Frederick C. Smith distanced himself from the debacle and assured citizens that he did not order the raid. In a statement released the next day, he called the raid "an insult to those present in the theatre as well as those who have been taking part in the sweepstakes, which means the public at large."[280] He called it "a purely political move," designed to make it appear as though he had ordered the raid in an attempt to thwart his reelection plans.[281] "And moreover," the mayor concluded, "if the police authorities really meant to enforce the ordinance against gambling they could have arrested everyone in the theater building, for the ordinance specifically commands this be done."[282]

During the Great Depression, the movie industry was in need of something to attract patrons. While theatres dropped ticket prices from twenty-five cents in 1929 to ten cents or lower during the 1930s, ticket prices could only drop so far. To entice patrons to the theatre, owners tried free dish night, free matinee tickets for ladies and even free hams. The most popular enticement was the sweepstakes.

Starting on May 7, 1936, the Marion Palace held a weekly Wednesday night sweepstakes, which Marion greatly enjoyed. In fact, as the Palace attorneys gleefully pointed out, two city police officers had registered in the past for the sweepstakes, as had the chief of police's daughter.[283]

In the Palace sweepstakes, patrons were given free sweepstakes tickets with the names of horses on them. They signed their names and put their addresses on the blank portions of the tickets and handed those portions back for the later drawing. A patron could get the ticket at the Palace at any time the box office was open. The ticket had to be kept for presentation inside the theatre on sweepstakes night. It was not necessary to purchase a

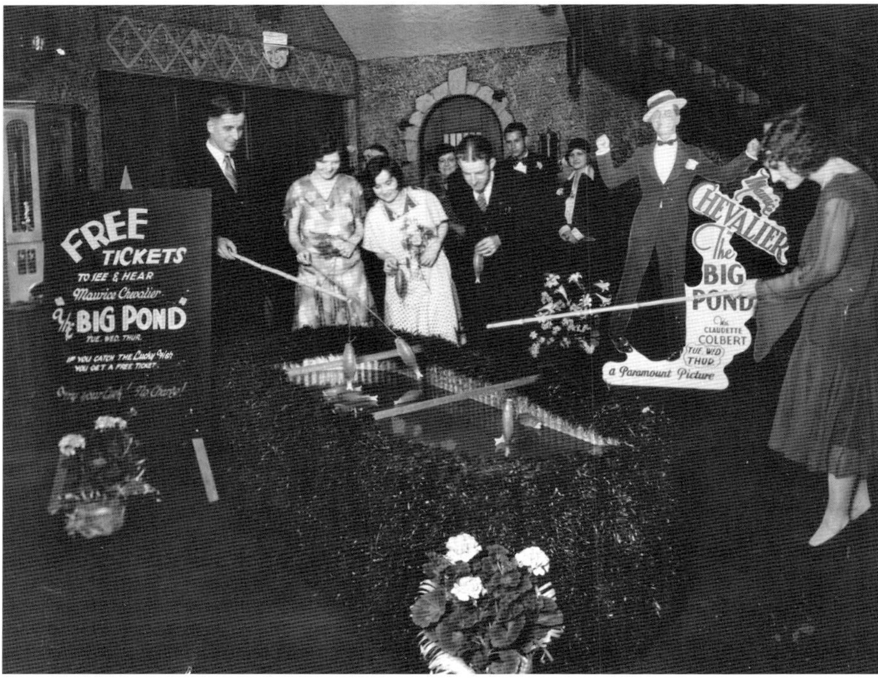

Theatres tried different types of incentives to compete for movie patrons. To promote *The Big Pond*, patrons could fish for a free ticket to see the movie, exhibited on May 13–15, 1930. *Courtesy of the Marion County Historical Society.*

movie ticket or to be inside the theatre when the winner was announced. Patrons could wait outside the theatre and listen to the stage announcements through an outside speaker. If their ticket matched what was called on stage, they simply entered the theatre without any need to purchase a ticket.[284]

The Palace management was careful to comply with the state anti-lottery prohibition. Eight months before the raid, Planck had met with Marks and Mayor Smith and discussed the sweepstakes. Planck assured both men that the sweepstakes was legal and that he was happy to discuss it with them at any time. A raid on the Palace, or his arrest, would never be necessary, Planck told both men.[285]

The trial was held on September 8 and 9, 1937.[286] A jury heard testimony that on the night of the raid, a plainclothes police officer was stationed inside, where he could observe the nefarious acts and then allow other officers inside.[287] Police burst in from three separate doors—six officers entered through the two west doors, and two entered through the main lobby doors—at the moment the

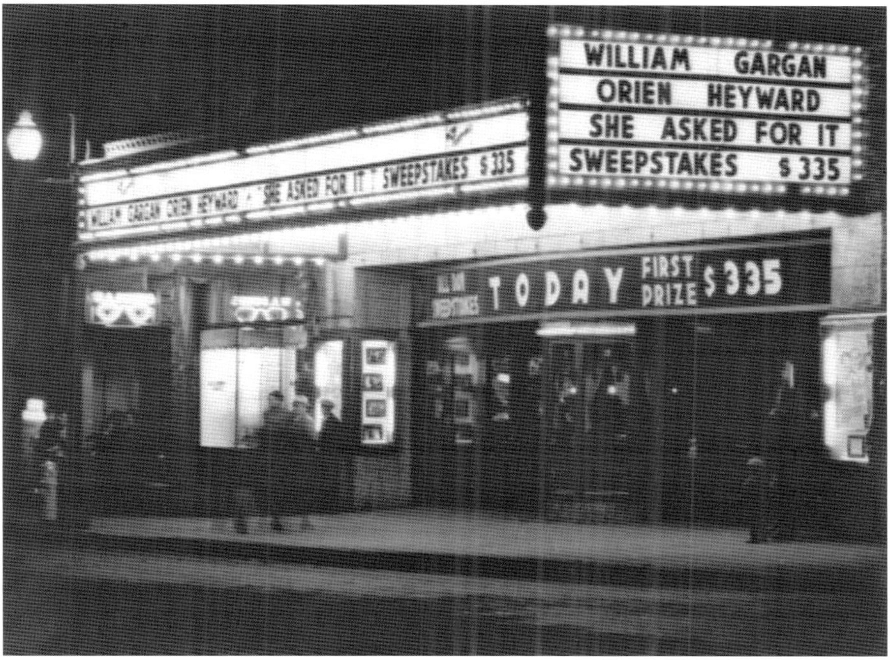

The Palace marquee and signs above the lobby doors advertised a $335 first prize. The sweepstakes survived a legal challenge. *Courtesy of the Palace Cultural Arts Association. Gift of Karl Stewart Estate.*

sweepstakes game reached the dramatic announcement of the winner.[288] Officers went to the stage and to the projection room to seize evidence.[289] Outside, two additional officers managed traffic while the parade of Marion police officers and the arrested Palace employees crossed West Center Street to headquarters.[290]

Testimony was given about how the sweepstakes was conducted.[291] On sweepstakes night, up to twenty sweepstakes ticket stubs with names were drawn from a wire hopper on the stage. These twenty people became the finalists for that night.

There were two ways to win. On Wednesday, at the matinee, a patron could register his or her attendance with an employee. Then, on Wednesday nights—sweepstakes night—if that patron's ticket were picked from a wire hopper on the stage, the patron would automatically win the sweepstakes (or second or third place, depending on the order it was drawn). This encouraged matinee attendance.

If there were no matinee winners (or fewer than three), then the remaining finalists were eligible to win. The finalists looked at their tickets to see which horse's name appeared. Next, someone came to the stage and chose a film from a stack of four films, each showing a horse race. This film was taken to the projection booth and was shown to determine the winner of the horse race. The audience watched the race to see if any of the finalists held a ticket with a horse that came in first, second or third. The order of finish in the horse race movie determined the winner of the first ($200), second ($10) and third ($5) sweepstakes prizes. To win, the patron had to have been one of the twenty finalists selected that night and had to hold a ticket with the name of the horse that finished first, second or third in the race. The sweepstakes winners had three minutes to get to the Palace stage. If the winner was not in the theatre or didn't make it to the stage from outside within the three-minute time limit, the prize accumulated for the next week. The prize also accumulated for the next week if no one held a winning ticket.

That night there was a finalist who held a ticket with the name of the horse that won the race in the movie shown. Just as the winner was announced, the police burst into the theatre. The woman who won the $200 reportedly left the theatre in disappointment. "That's my money and they know it!"[292]

The judge ruled that the sweepstakes was an illegal lottery and left it to the jury to determine whether Planck had been responsible for conducting it.[293] In only seventeen minutes, the jury returned a unanimous not guilty verdict.[294] Confusion ensued as the lawyers tussled about whether the jury had the right to determine that the sweepstakes was legal. Carhart decided to seek a new trial, but the city council ended the matter by denying Carhart's request for the fifty-dollar fee to appeal the case.[295] Leaving nothing to chance, the council also voted that all seized equipment would be immediately returned to the Palace. Marks and Carhart may have been the loneliest two men in town. Meanwhile, Planck wasted no time in resuming the sweepstakes.[296]

PART VI

MARION'S THEATRES

11

THE OTHER THEATRES

The Palace was by no means Marion's first theatre.[297] Even the old city hall was used as a performance venue. Starting in the late nineteenth century, Marion was large enough to attract traveling entertainments. Well into the twentieth century, minstrel shows, circuses, vaudeville shows, plays and musical concerts came to the city to perform in halls and tents.

While many Marion residents welcomed options for entertainment, others worried about its effect on the health and welfare of the city. A few just didn't see the wisdom of spending money on a vaudeville act or moving picture. In 1906, the *Marion Daily Star* summarized it this way:

> *Of course, all these places mean that the people of Marion are finding it much easier to spend their money than was the case in years gone by. Still, the list of boarders at the county infirmary is no longer than ordinary, and the patrons of these places of amusement seem to be eating as much and wearing as good clothes as ever. The general impression seems to be that there is a great deal of profit to be found in an evening passed in some place where good moral entertainment is to be found, and that the man who stays at home every night and rubs his hard-earned coin until the polish turns to a dull, sickly hue, is missing half his life.*[298]

Over Marion's history, there were enough coins leaving pockets to support a long list of theatres.

ARONHOLT GROUNDS (1870s–1943)

Aronholt Grounds, located on North Prospect Street, was the site for traveling theatre troupes, which pitched tents there during the summer months.[299] One popular company was Kinsey Komedy Kompany, a family business that toured Ohio and other states. A branch of the Kinsey family split from the business in 1935 and formed the Madge Kinsey Players. Both repertory companies made appearances at the Arnholt Grounds and other sites in Marion.[300] It was also the site for many circus events in Marion, including Barnum and Bailey Circus (1897) and Buffalo Bill (1900).

APOLLO HALL / BENNETT HALL (1880–1882)

Apollo Hall was used as an early Marion theatre. It was located on the third floor of the Bennett Building (on the site now occupied by the Union Bank Company). Performances were held there as early as November 1880, including the popular *Uncle Tom's Cabin* in November of that year.[301] In the spring of 1882, the stage was removed and a new floor installed for dances.[302] By then, all indoor stage productions had moved to city hall.

CITY HALL (1870s–1890s)

In the decades of the 1870s through the 1890s, Marion's city hall was used as a theatre.[303] It was located at the northeast corner of South and West Streets (Church and Prospect Streets), now a parking lot across from the Presbyterian church. Performances were managed by the town marshal. A local citizen, Edward Moore, posted the advertising bills around town and also acted as house manager. Theatrical companies rented a large hall in the building for productions, keeping the box office receipts. Some companies were brought to Marion by local citizens, who rented the hall and then shared the receipts with the traveling actors.

Seating was uncomfortable but not unusual for the time. A combination of wooden chairs and long wooden benches was used. None was cushioned, unless a patron brought a pillow. Row numbers were marked in chalk on the

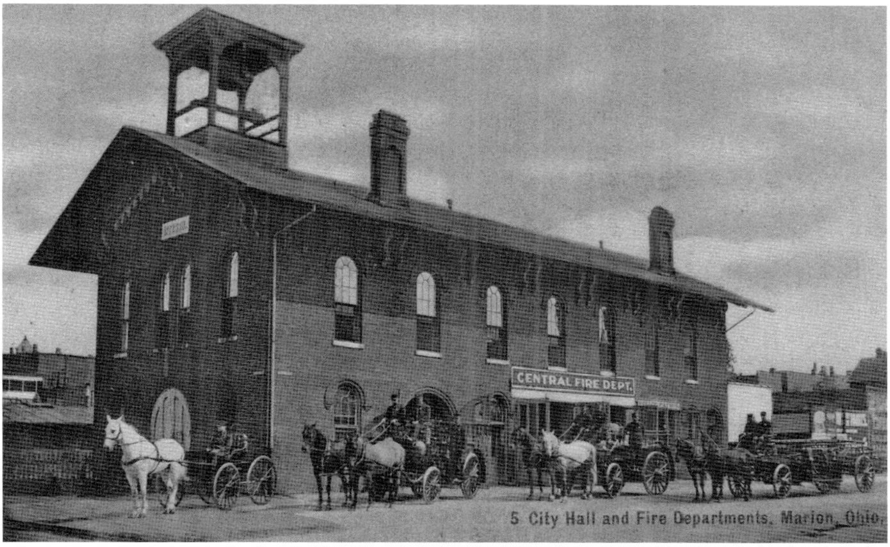

A 1908 postcard view of the Marion City Hall and Fire Department. Built in 1857, the city hall's second floor was the venue for many concerts and theatrical events. It was also the home of the "police patrol" (entrance to the right of the Central Fire Department sign). *Author's collection.*

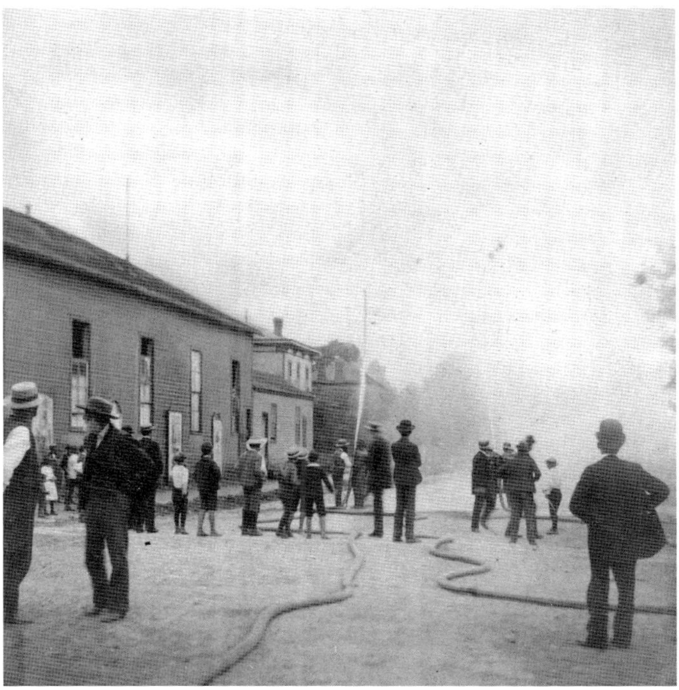

Music Hall (the Wigwam), at left, as it appeared in 1890. The view is at Church and Prospect Streets, looking north. The white spray is the result of the men in the photo who are testing the pressure of the newly installed fire hydrants. *Courtesy of the Mike and Linda Perry Collection.*

floor, and numbers were placed on the seats, also with chalk. Raised seats were provided in the gallery at the rear.

For the actors, comfort was minimal. Only two dressing rooms were provided. Other cast members dressed in stairwells or wherever space could be found. Lighting, drops and scenery were minimal, unless the touring company brought its own. The stage curtain contained advertisements by local businesses, which helped defray general costs of the city in providing an entertainment space.

The earliest known performance was on October 12, 1877, when the Wallace Sisters dramatic company performed to a packed audience. Admission was $0.50 ($11.50 in 2014 dollars). Many performers played at city hall, including Lizzie Evans, a famous vaudeville and musical theatre star from Mount Vernon.

City hall was a primitive performance space. On January 31, 1880, the *Marion Daily Star* reported that the building would no longer be used for theatre "until it is put in order."[304] Due to the condition of the building, people were unwilling to attend. The paper noted that "no theater has made a cent that has visited our city for some time." On February 2, 1880, it was announced that the railway company could run excursion trains to Prospect until a new opera house was completed. The closure was short-lived. On March 16, 1880, city hall was back in business with the Hotto Comedy Company performing for one week.[305] City hall space continued to be used into the 1890s, but only on rare occasions. The new Music Hall provided a new, more permanent theatre.

MUSIC HALL, THE "WIGWAM" (1883–1893)

Music Hall, Marion's first building constructed specifically for entertainment, was located at the northwest corner of South and West Streets (now Church and Prospect Streets), opposite Marion's old city hall. The building was affectionately referred to as the "Wigwam"—its nickname came from the oval auditorium and cone-shaped roof. It was a large frame building, fifty-six by ninety-four feet in dimension.[306] The building was owned by a local company of which George B. Christian was president; C.C. Pettit, secretary; and G.R. James, treasurer.[307]

Entertainment and public meetings of all kinds were held there. Seating capacity was eight hundred people on the main floor and four hundred in the galleries.[308] In the 1880s, it was said that the theatre had a stage (twenty-eight by fifty feet) and scenery equal to that of a first-class theatre in the cities.[309] Four dressing rooms were constructed.[310]

Some were disappointed. The Music Hall was not a comfortable substitute for the grand opera house that Marion had long awaited. Seating was provided on wooden chairs and long wooden benches. The walls were plain, unadorned with decoration. But for a city with a population of four thousand people (the county's population was twenty-one thousand), it was a start—certainly better than city hall.

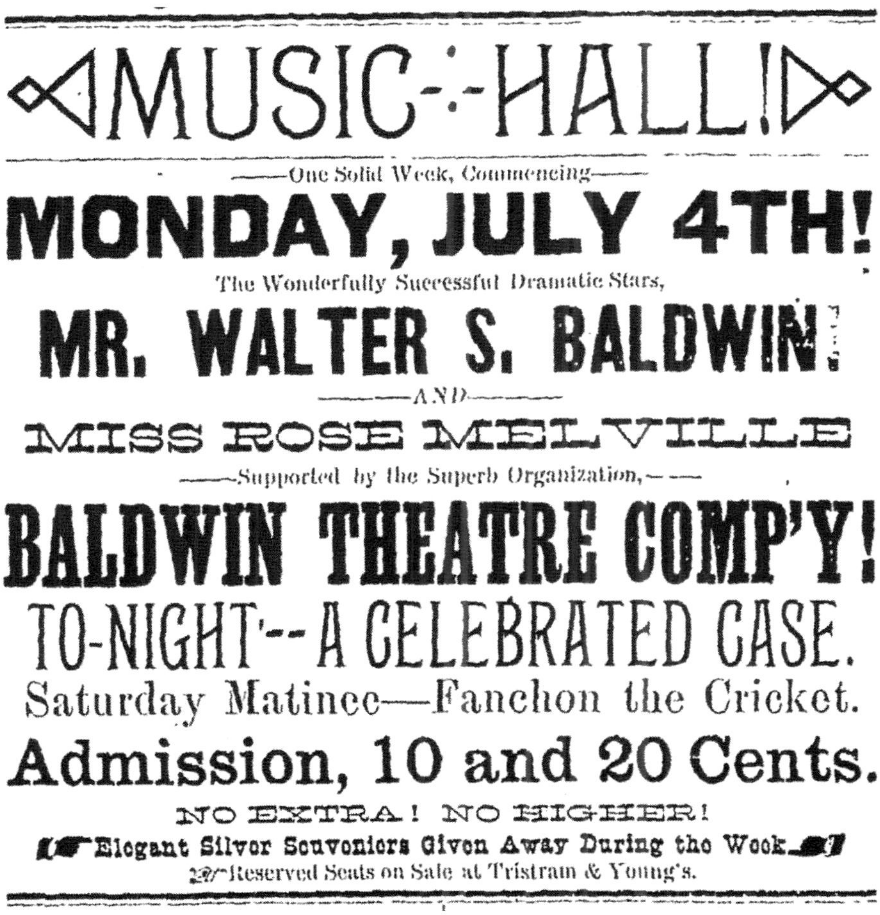

MUSIC HALL!

—One Solid Week, Commencing—

MONDAY, JULY 4TH!

The Wonderfully Successful Dramatic Stars,

MR. WALTER S. BALDWIN

—AND—

MISS ROSE MELVILLE

—Supported by the Superb Organization,—

BALDWIN THEATRE COMP'Y!

TO-NIGHT—A CELEBRATED CASE.

Saturday Matinee—Fanchon the Cricket.

Admission, 10 and 20 Cents.

NO EXTRA! NO HIGHER!

Elegant Silver Souvenirs Given Away During the Week

Reserved Seats on Sale at Tristram & Young's.

A July 4, 1887 *Marion Daily Star* advertisement for the Music Hall. *Courtesy of the* Marion Daily Star.

Although not completely finished inside, the Music Hall opened on May 29, 1883, with a community production of *The Drummer Boy of Shiloh*.[311] Performed for five nights, it was the first of many community productions at the Music Hall. At the time, Civil War–related theatre was very popular. *The Drummer Boy of Shiloh* was second in popularity only to the play *Uncle Tom's Cabin* and was steadily performed for forty years throughout the North. Tickets were thirty-five cents for general admission. The NYP&O Railway and the Kenton and Upper Sandusky Railway advertised special rates for the opening.[312]

The Music Hall formally opened three months later, on August 30, 1883, with a well-known star, Harry Lacy, appearing in the play *The Planter's Wife*.[313] The company was booked on its way from New York City to Cincinnati and was promised a guaranteed box office share of $350 ($8,400 in 2014 dollars) if it stopped and performed in Marion.[314]

Some of the acts that performed there were as bad as the seats. Samuel Smith, a stagehand at the Wigwam, provided the *Marion Daily Star* with a recollection of some of the acts that played there.[315] Smith said that the worst play at the Wigwam was *Aunt Betsy's Trial*. He said that it was so bad that when the audience got up to leave, frightened actors thought they were going to attack.

On April 1, 1893, the lease for the land on which the Wigwam was built expired.[316] It was demolished on June 28, 1893, to make room for the construction of the First Presbyterian Church.[317] Until 1896, when the Grand Opera House opened its doors, Marion was without a theatre. During that time, traveling companies brought tents for performances or appeared at city hall. Otherwise, residents traveled to Columbus and other nearby cities to see shows.

GERMANIA PARK HALL (1895–1902)

A park pavilion and beer garden owned by George Ackerman provided entertainment for residents beginning sometime in 1895. Traveling theatre troupes performed on the stage, as did Marion's German band. Nearby residents were displeased with the location of the pavilion. They pressed the mayor for a 10:00 p.m. closing time and proper screening of the area.[318] Eventually, the opposition diminished as the pavilion became popular as a place for dances and theatre.

After the Music Hall closed, it was difficult to attract quality shows to Marion, especially those that appealed to the German-speaking population.

In 1897, Ackerman hired Bryan Spaun, a vaudeville performer, to manage the pavilion. The venue was then referred to as Germania Park Hall.[319] For his first bookings, Spaun retained acrobatic comedians Sully and Moore; Lottie Hart, a soubrette who sang "up-to-date" songs; balladist Violet Page; and Spaun performing "his original specialty acts entitled the 'Rube from Studenville.'"[320] Marion was assured that the actors would provide a "first class and refined vaudeville performance, of clean character."[321] At the time, these words meant that women and children could attend.

The hall also served as a place for balls, at least one of which ended in a fight. On February 10, 1898, someone had made a remark to a woman that she didn't like, and she gave him an uppercut that sent him off the porch. The *Star* reported that no one was hurt seriously: "It was simply one of those little unavoidable annoyances that occur in this class of society. They never result in anything worse than murder, but of course are deeply regretted by the murdered man's friends."[322]

Entertainment at the hall ended in 1902, although there were dances held occasionally. The building was leased to Gebhardt Piano Company for six months in 1902, as temporary space until its new building was finished.[323] After that, the hall had a seedy history that included an illegal prizefight in 1916.[324]

GRAND OPERA HOUSE (1896–1910)

On October 25, 1877, the *Daily Star* printed a short request to its readers. "It is about time Marion is building a [*sic*] Opera house as City Hall is altogether too small."[325] The following year, on March 6, 1878, the *Daily Star* called for an opera house that would seat "2,000 people, at least."[326] The next month, the newspaper cajoled leaders about the "great and pressing need" for an opera house, citing the presence of six different theatre troupes that morning, all looking for a place to show.[327] Finally, after months of prodding by the *Daily Star*, a meeting was held on December 2, 1878, to discuss an opera house. The announcement of the meeting appeared in the *Daily Star* and was signed by forty-four local residents, including Richard Fahey, Henry True and George B. Christian.[328]

The day of the meeting, a letter to the editor was printed that attempted to direct the anticipated discussion away from a tax increase to build the opera house. The writer counseled that the motto for the meeting should be: "Let those who want one pay for it, and let all contribute who can."[329]

Warning of the perils of high taxes, the writer attributed Marion's prosperity to its low taxes, while neighboring towns were so debt-ridden that anyone in a position to sell did so and left town.[330] The letter was unsigned.

Meeting attendees were unanimous in a vote to organize a joint stock company to build Marion's first opera house.[331] Donations would also be accepted from those who did not want, or lacked funds, to purchase stock. It was to be a community effort, and no one was to be excluded.[332] Before the meeting ended, Amos H. Kling, a strict capitalist and one of Marion's wealthiest citizens, couldn't allow the meeting to end without assurances that taxes would not be raised. "Resolved," he said, "that in no event will this meeting endorse any proposition looking to taxation for the purpose of having the money expended in erecting an 'Opera House,' or any building for such purpose."[333] There was no second to his motion, and the meeting was adjourned.[334] If the stock could be subscribed, Marion would have its first Opera House.

Efforts to raise capital and obtain land in exchange for stock were a failure. The long depression of 1873–79 didn't help provide optimism for an investment in amusement. For most of the businessmen who supported the idea of an opera house, they did so as a long-term investment in the community, not as a solid financial investment. Theatres were risky, and Marion's population of fewer than three thousand made the financial success questionable.

On June 8, 1880, the *Marion Daily Star* published a short list of events that would happen when the world came to an end. Frustrated by the lack of progress, the newspaper quipped that the world would probably end just as the opera house foundation was completed.[335] By 1883, no progress had been made, but at least Marion had the Wigwam, which opened that year.

Like he did with so many improvements that were for the good of Marion, editor Warren G. Harding (he purchased the *Marion Daily Star* in 1884) decided to use his newspaper to press for a new opera house.[336] His writing style made the point with characteristic humor, tempered with political restraint. In a February 18, 1889 article, he noted that Marion was waiting for a new train depot, a new railroad and a new opera house. Calling these "the things-that-do-not-come," Harding seemed even willing to settle for a raised floor and cushioned seats at the Wigwam.[337] If even that were not possible, Harding joked that amusement-loving Marionites would become a race of "craned-necks and calloused-rumps."[338]

On April 18, 1891, Harding's *Marion Daily Star* warned that if Marion's "monied men" did not invest for the good of Marion in a new opera house, a vote to build one would pass.[339] Beginning with the first talk about an opera house in 1878, use of tax money for funding had been opposed by Amos H. Kling, Harding's father-in-law (Harding married Florence Kling on July 8, 1891). As if speaking directly to Kling, one of the city's most significant "monied men," the paper warned that those who disagreed could take note of the editorial and await the outcome. Kling opposed Harding's marriage to his daughter, and Harding perhaps took out some of his frustration with Kling in his paper, disguised as a comment on tax policy.

The editorial came only a year before it was announced that the Wigwam would close. On April 28, 1892, the Presbyterian Church voted to buy the site of the Music Hall and demolish it for a new church building.[340] This left Marion without a theatre. The monied men were now faced with a tax increase to build an opera house, which some worried would pass, or using their own capital in a dubious investment.

They bought time. A YMCA and two new church buildings needed to be funded, and the city's investors lacked the resources to undertake the additional financial requirements of the opera house project. Or so they said. Marion would have to be patient, they hoped. The *Star*, unwilling to argue the merits of an opera house versus the other three buildings, merely noted in a May 4, 1892 column that "we have already learned patience."[341]

Finally, on March 9, 1895, the newspaper announced the "cheerful news."[342] J.J. Hane, Amos H. Kling and Edward Huber, men of "ample means and abundant local pride," would build a "first class" opera house.[343] It would be located on the 100 block of State Street at the site of the Dunt family house.[344] A total of 1,086 seats would be included, with a large standing-room section. The designs also included several boxes.

A stage sixty-one feet wide and thirty-five feet deep was designed to accommodate large productions. Eight dressing rooms below the stage and two star dressing rooms in the fly area just above the stage were planned. Two retail store spaces were planned for the front of the building, facing State Street, one on each side of the building. The second floor was designed for residential housing. A ballroom was designed for the third floor, with thirty-eight by forty-nine feet of clear floor space.

Meanwhile, meetings were held to finalize details on who would own the opera house and how it would be funded. The original incorporators were leading Marion businessmen. They were J.J. Hane, Amos H. Kling, J.F. Prendergast, J.J. Hopkins, Wesley Harsch, F.S. Keiler, B.E. Kleimaier, J.G. Leffler, G.H. Kling, J.L. Elliott, Harvey Wilson, Edward Huber, Henry Strelitz, C.C. Stoltz, G. Lefller, J.A. Wolford, F.R. Saiter, G.W. King, H. Ackerman, N. Mezger, T.J. McMurray and E. Durfee. Selling the stock was not a problem, since by that time most had already made the decision to contribute the money.

Designed by Pittsburg architect William Kauffman, the exterior of the Colonial-style building was unlike any other in Marion.[345] The first floor was finished with red sandstone and the second and third with buff-colored brick and intricately designed terra cotta. Granite columns supported a wide entrance arch. Entrance doors with beveled glass were decorated in green and gold gilt.

The *Marion Daily Star* described to its readers the "neat, tasty and elegant" theatre:

> *The lobby is itself a picture. To the outside of the portals a light wainscoting is shown in perfect imitation of Scandinavian sienna marble while in the lobby proper the wainscoting is in imitation of the now almost-priceless Numidian marble. Above this wainscoting the decorator has excelled himself and has given to the lobby the best possible effects in red gilt and green.*
>
> *Traversing the lobby the visitor passes the ticket office, to the left, and to the right the entrance to the second story offices, and enters the foyer of the theatre, which presents in bronze green and brown the evidence of a most masterly decorative art.*
>
> *Here the perfect beauty of the interior of the house presents itself. To the right and left are retiring rooms and stairways leading to the floors above, while looking ahead under the carelessly draped curtains the spectator catches sight of the dress circle, the parquet and the stage with the four boxes at either side.*
>
> *The entire house is furnished with Abbey theater chairs, the very finest on the market, the first thirteen rows on the lower level, the parquet, and the first three rows of the balcony being upholstered in red silk plush, the nine rows in the dress circle being finished in mahogany and the remainder of the house the same style.*
>
> *The eight boxes, four of which are closed, one above and one below on either side, and two open boxes above on either side are seated with chairs of willow and in fine gilt and are like the foyer and the lower floor and balcony aisles carpeted with a heavy body Brussels of a rich bottle green, through which is shown a trace of terracotta.*
>
> *Ascending to the balcony the perfection of the mural decoration is fully realized and right here it may be stated that the superb beauty and artistic excellence of the mural decorations make the house to a notable degree, the success which it is.*

> *The color theme is terracotta, ivory and gold, and the style Romanesque, and it simply defies the power of the pen to tell of the beautiful lights and shadings and color effects which the mural decorator has attained. The side walls, the ceiling and especially its central decoration and the proscenium arch in fact the entire house bespeaks the artist's worth.*
>
> *The entire house is lighted by both gas and electricity and the lighting could not be in any way improved upon as it is simply perfect.*
>
> *Behind the drop curtain a large and roomy stage gives ample room for the use of any scenery carried by the largest traveling companies while the house affords many sets of scenery of most excellent quality. At the Wednesday night performance only two complete sets were shown, a French chamber scene and a street scene, but there are, among many others of merit, a cut wood scene and a mountain scene, the artistic excellence of which cannot be questioned. The excellence of the drop curtain may be questioned but the stage scenery proper, is unquestionably fine and does credit to the artist.*
>
> *To the rear of the closed boxes are tiers of rooms to be used as dressing rooms and property rooms, while below the stage are ten dressing rooms, the green room, and the many contrivances for performances.*
>
> *Above the stage is, of course, the gridiron and the scene-shifters gallery and throughout the entire portion of the house to the rear of the curtain the electric lights are so arranged that a flood of white, red or green light or a combination of any two, can be turned on at will giving sunrise, sunset, mid-day or moonlight effects of the very finest.*[346]

The newspaper that had waited so long for the opera house concluded that it was a "perfect gem of a theatre."[347]

The Grand Opera House opened its doors on August 19, 1896. Hortense Rhéa (1844–1899), a Belgian-born French actress, entertained Marion that night and the next. She toured throughout America during her stage career and was extremely popular in the Midwest. In fact, she had appeared once before in Marion, in *Much Ado About Nothing* at the Wigwam. The program on opening night included her performance in the four-act play *Nell Gwynne*. On the second night, she performed the title role in *Josephine, Empress of the French.*

Not long after the opening, it became clear that the new opera house was a money-losing venture—so unsuccessful, in fact, that Amos Kling was no longer a shareholder. Sheriff Battenfeld found this out when he served a legal notice on Kling in a lawsuit by the Grand Opera House Orchestra in which it demanded payment. Kling was "uproariously angered."[348] He told the Sheriff that he was out of the investment and "glad of it."[349] The *Star*

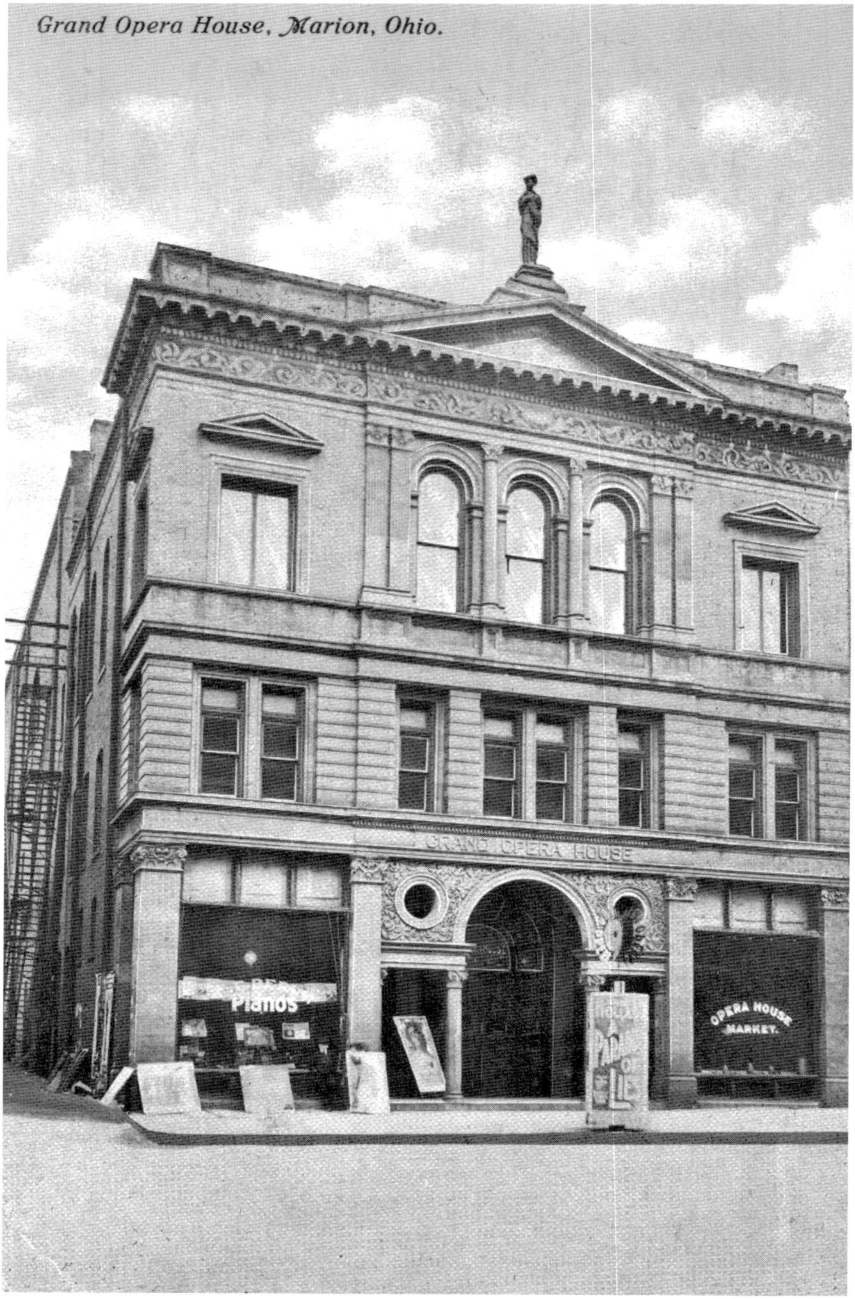

A postcard showing the Grand Opera House, circa 1906. *Courtesy of the Mike and Linda Perry Collection.*

reported that Kling told the sheriff that there were "deadbeats" in Marion "bleeding" the opera house of money.[350] Kling concluded this unhappy encounter by telling the sheriff to go to the "demnition bowwows" with the lawsuit and the opera house.[351] (In 1898, that meant: "damn dogs.") The sheriff replied that he would have to close the opera house. Kling, always accustomed to having the last word, replied (perhaps prophetically) that he didn't care if the sheriff burned it.[352]

On September 1, 1898, the fortunes of the Grand Opera House brightened. Charles E. Perry became the manager and lessee. It was an arrangement that lasted almost as long as the Grand Opera House stood. The owners became so confident with Perry's management that in 1906 he was granted a five-year lease at $4,000 a year.[353] In doing so, the rent Perry had paid under his old lease was increased by $1,500 a year, surpassing bidders from Toledo, Bellefontaine and Philadelphia.[354] Perry was confident about his prospects also and enjoyed a good relationship with other businessmen in Marion. To supplement theatre receipts, he opened a music store in one of the two opera house retail stores.

Three years later, Perry left the Grand Opera House. What happened to him is uncertain. All that appears in the newspapers of the year is that he left Marion to relocate somewhere in the western United States.[355] With the increased rent he agreed to pay and his new music business, he may have been overextended. Whatever the reason, he departed Marion.

From the beginning, the Grand Opera House lost money. While it was called one of the most beautiful in the state, and although top talent was being booked, ticket sales never justified sufficient rent to pay dividends to shareholders. Even before Charles Perry left, the remaining investors wanted out. Shareholder M.J. Sullivan, an oil and natural gas investor, worked on a solution that he believed would improve the possibilities for success. To do so, he had to oppose some of the most powerful men in Marion.

Sullivan secured options on large blocks of Grand Opera House Company stock. His plan was to purchase the rest of the stock and transfer ownership to a new company. He offered the other stockholders a purchase price of ten cents on the dollar. In a January 23, 1906 article, the *Marion Daily Star* reported that the minority shareholders had met and voted to decline the offer.[356] Even though the company had lost money and never paid a dividend, the shareholders were hopeful that lease renegotiations of the rental space would result in a profit and decided to try to hang on to their shares.[357] But Sullivan controlled 52 percent of the shares. The control of the Grand was his.[358]

It was a public fight that revealed a change in the civility of the leaders of Marion. Few of the men who had contributed money to build it did so with the primary interest of making a profit. Rather, the corporation was organized and funded out of a sense of duty to contribute to the success of Marion. George W. King, who had founded the Marion Power Shovel Company with Henry Barnhart and Edward Huber, was not happy with Sullivan and his takeover. For King, who had invested in the opera house because it was good for Marion, it was a slap in the face:

> *But, in addition to this* [poor financial performance] *and far more important, some of us are disposed to look at this matter with much more seriousness than the mere financial transaction would warrant. It shows the breaking up of a long-established principle among Marion's business men. In the past, when associating themselves together for any undertaking, it was generally understood that they would stand or fall together, no difference whether the scheme proved to be a success or failure. All stockholders, large or small, shared alike. This principle was established by our late and dear friend, Mr. Edward Huber, the man that was instrumental in building Marion from a mere village to a thriving manufacturing city. The crowning feature of his success was his high regard for the rights and interests of his business associates, as well as the general welfare of Marion…While we have endeavored to protect our friends, some have neglected to consider our mutual interests. But, be the outcome what it may, it is to be hoped that the future management will give entertainments that will be thoroughly satisfactory to Marion's best citizens. Respectfully, George W. King.*[359]

For good or bad, the age of the old guard's good-intentioned paternalism was coming to an end.

A few years later, the opera house was gone. In what was estimated as a $100,000 loss by the *Marion Daily Star*[360] and $65,000 by the *Marion Daily Mirror*, an early morning fire on December 6, 1910, completely destroyed the building and its contents.[361] The *Marion Daily Mirror* reported that the fire was discovered by an employee of United Electric Co., an electric supply store that leased a storefront space in the building. When she opened the door for the morning business, the draft caused the room to fill with smoke. She escaped the store and called the central office, which then contacted the fire department.[362]

Inside the building were two tenants, the Muscat family—husband, wife and three children—and Roy Miller, the building custodian. Both

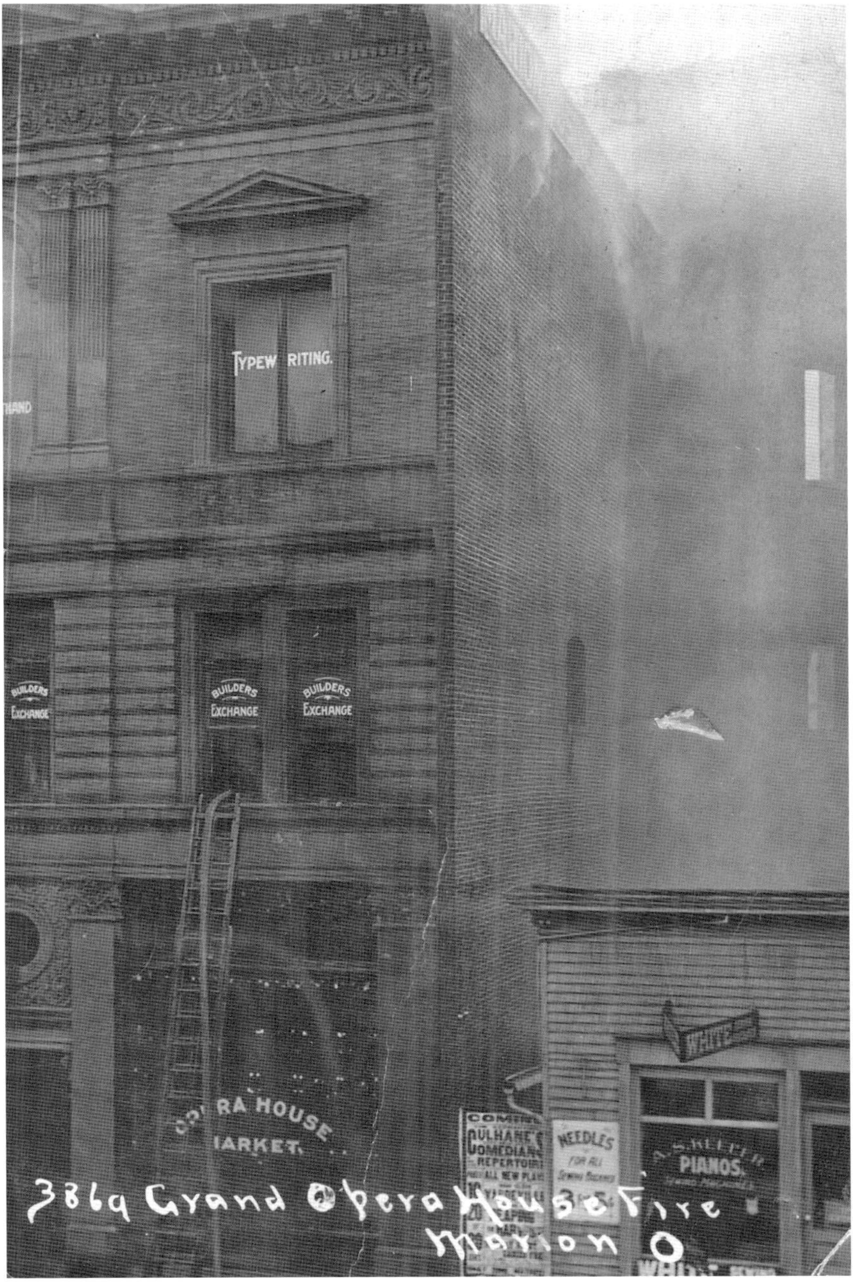

The Grand Opera House fire, December 6, 1910. Firefighters use a ladder to enter the building. To the right is a sign advertising Culhane's Comedians, who lost their costumes and sets in the fire. *Courtesy of the Mike and Linda Perry Collection.*

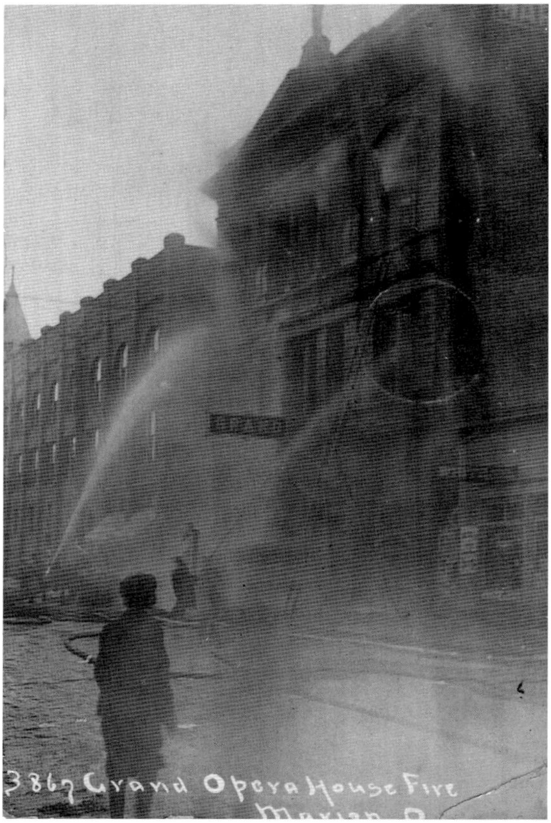

Left: Firefighters began to spray water on the burning Grand Opera House. Initial thoughts were that the fire could be controlled and would not spread beyond the front of the building. *Courtesy of the Mike and Linda Perry Collection.*

Below: The fire soon engulfed the auditorium and stage. The F.E. Stengel optician office is in the foreground. *Courtesy of the Mike and Linda Perry Collection.*

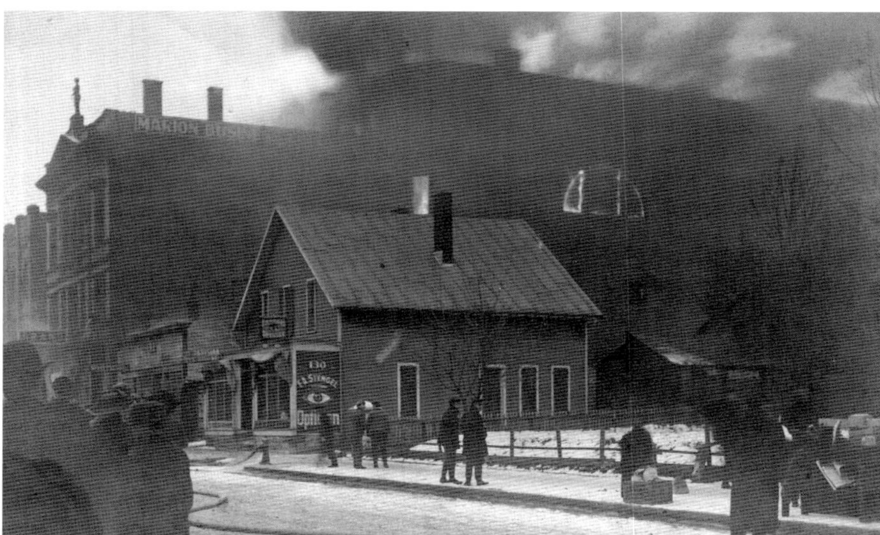

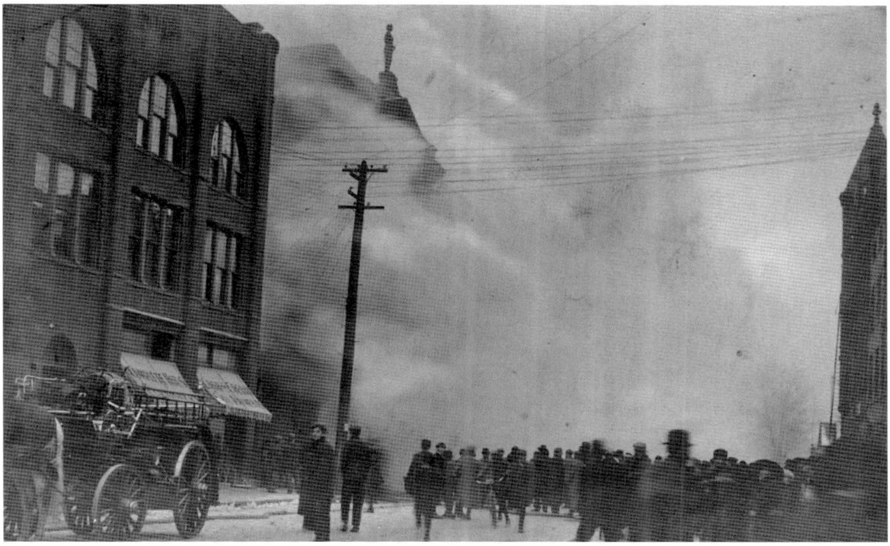

Above: A horse-drawn fire truck (left) is parked away from the fire. Smoke filled the street as spectators gathered in the early morning cold. By this point, the fire was no longer under control. *Courtesy of the Mike and Linda Perry Collection.*

Right: Smoke continued to come from the building, and all attempts to save anything inside were abandoned. *Courtesy of the Mike and Linda Perry Collection.*

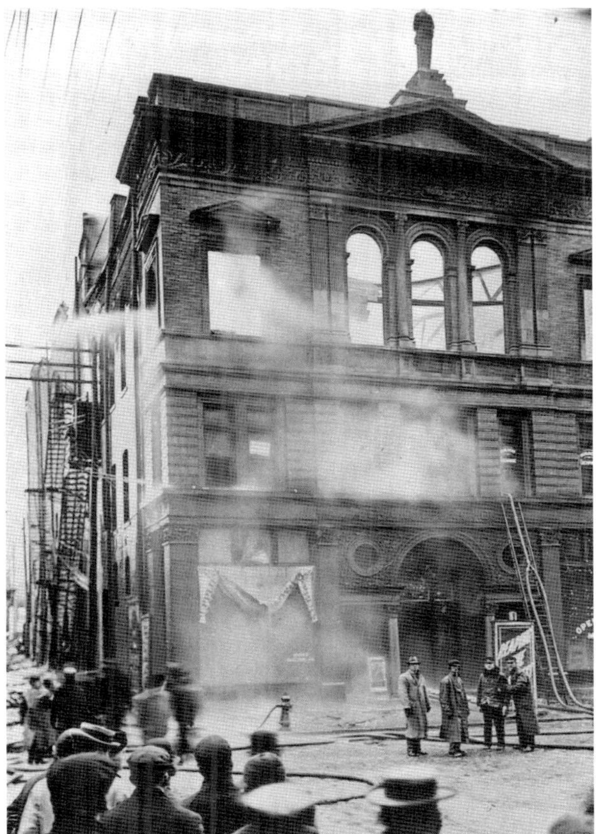

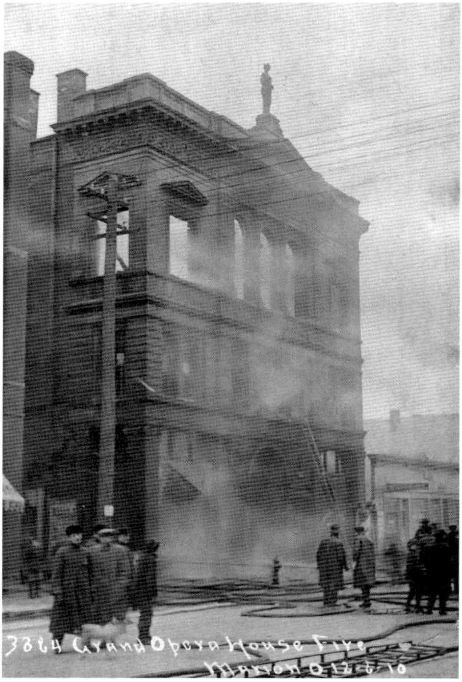

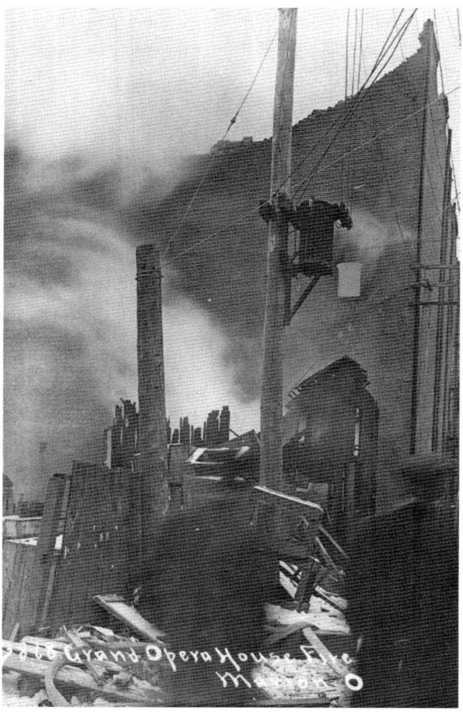

occupied different flats on the second floor. Mr. Muscat, who lived in the north flat, had awakened to the smell of burning wood and rushed to help his family escape as the rear of the flat filled with smoke. He called Miller, who quickly dressed and used a fire escape to go to the street to call for the fire department.[363]

The fire intensified so quickly that the family's only escape route was up to the third floor and down a fire escape. The *Marion Daily Star* reported:

> *Muscat directed his wife and three children to follow him to the fire escape and went in advance of them. He reached the fire escape, but his wife and three children were unable to find their way through the dense smoke and returned to the front part of the house, opening a window. In going to the front room, Mrs. Muscat lost her daughter, Beatrice, a girl of eleven years,*

Top: Shopkeepers, officeworkers and bystanders began to leave for work. The early morning fire had halted the morning routines of many. *Courtesy of the Mike and Linda Perry Collection.*

Left: A sidewall view shows that the roof is completely gone and bricks have fallen from the top of the wall. *Courtesy of the Mike and Linda Perry Collection.*

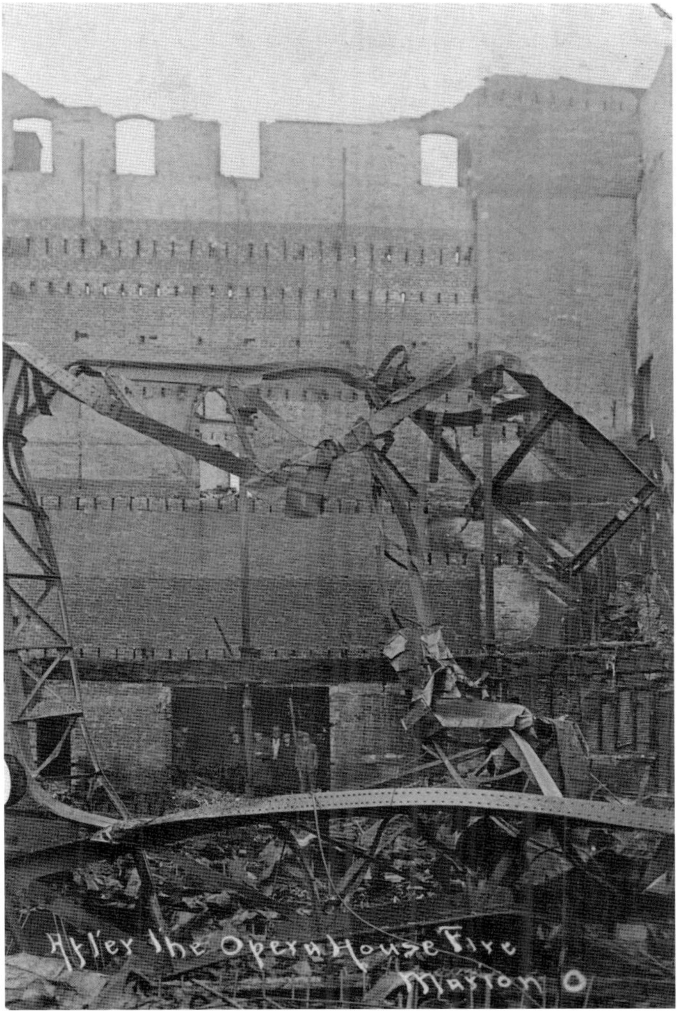

Inside the building, the auditorium and stage are completely gone. The fire was so hot that the steel beams were bent and twisted like straw. *Courtesy of the Mike and Linda Perry Collection.*

and returned to the kitchen in search of her. The three children were then placed on the sill of the window and with the mother were rescued in their night clothing by the firemen.

As it developed their plan of escape proved better than that of Muscat. When he reached the fire escape the flames were pouring out of two of the windows leading to the gallery stairs. Several times he started down the

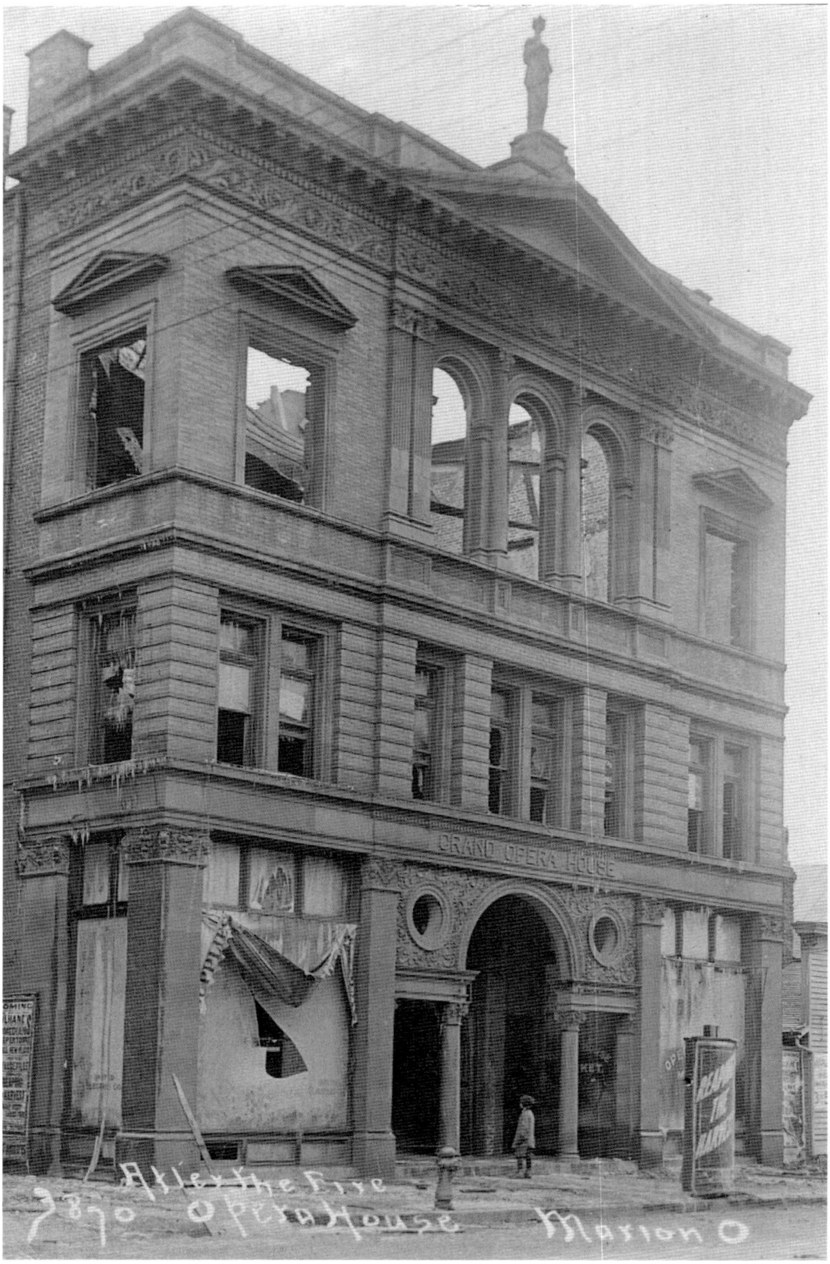

The day after the fire, a child surveyed the loss. A sign advertised a play, *Reaping the Harvest.* After a bitter battle for control, some may have seen this as foretelling a twist of fate. *Courtesy of the Mike and Linda Perry Collection.*

> *iron stairs and was driven back by the heat. His position, growing more perilous each moment and not being able to hear the advice given him from below, Muscat dashed down the fire escape, going through the flames from the window. When he reached the ground he was almost overcome by the smoke, heat and fright, while the location of his wife and children, whom he told to follow him, caused him great worry.*[364]

Mr. Muscat suffered a burned eye and arm. The family lost all of their possessions in the fire.

When the fire department arrived, the fire was confined to the front part of the building. By the time the water was turned on, the fire had eaten through the lower foyer to the balcony level. At one point, it appeared that the fire could be controlled and would not reach the stage.[365]

A theatre touring company, Culhane's Comedians of the Culhane Stock Company, tried to reach the stage to carry off their belongings, but dense smoke stopped them.[366] As soon as the fire reached the stage, the props, scenery, costumes and curtains were engulfed in flames. The loss of their stock was estimated at $25,000,[367] according to the *Star*, and up to $65,000, according to the *Mirror*.[368] The Marion Business College, which occupied the front of the third floor (formerly a dance hall), was lost.[369] The Grand Orchestra drummer lost his drums and traps.[370] The theatre manager lost his office furnishings and records.[371] Everything was gone.

Once the stage end of the building was consumed, the fire broke out again on the second and third floors, and then the roof fell in, parts of the south and west walls collapsed and the other walls sagged. When the fire reached the roof, flames shot up fifty feet, while officeworkers, schoolchildren and shopkeepers stared in disbelief. Red-hot iron beams twisted under the weight.[372] The fire department was helpless in putting out the fire, due to the highly flammable, scenery-filled stage and the low water pressure in the city. At one point, water pressure was so low that a fireman working on the roof of an adjacent building could not throw the water from his hose across the alley.[373]

Attention quickly turned to the cause of the fire.[374] The general consensus was that it started in the boiler room of the basement.[375] Speculation arose that a tramp had gained access through an unlocked door leading to the fire escape off the gallery.[376] It had been found unlocked before, and someone could have used that for access to the building and then used the basement as a place to sleep. That person could have caused an accidental fire. No definite cause could be determined.[377]

The twenty-seven stockholders (the *Marion Daily Star* said it was fifteen) lost almost all of their investment. The building was insured for a mere \$15,000.[378] Sullivan, who owned over \$25,000 in stock and a controlling interest, was despondent. Not only had he challenged the "monied men" for financial self-interest, but also he had lost it all in the end.[379]

ALHAMBRA THEATRE (GRAND THEATRE) (1914–30)

A new opera house was built by the local Elks lodge on the same lot where the Grand Opera House was destroyed by fire, using the original street façade. The Elks purchased the lot at a sheriff's sale on December 30, 1911, for \$15,000. The lodge immediately announced plans to rebuild the theatre and construct lodge quarters in the building.[380]

The rest of the year was spent raising funds for the construction, including a carnival. The carnival committee eventually paid \$10,000 of construction costs, made possible by attendance revenue and countless small donations of cakes, pies and other items.[381] Those fundraising efforts, together with a loan, provided the necessary funding for the new theatre.

Construction began in May 1913 after debris from the old opera house had been removed.[382] Formal construction approval was voted on August 7, 1913.[383] The 845-seat theatre, designed by architect Edward Elford of Columbus, opened on November 6, 1914.[384] Unlike its predecessor, the theatre was decorated in a "simplistic" style and painted in yellow with stenciling.[385] Dark green velvet carpet was installed in the aisles and staircases, and buff and white decorations were used throughout the theatre.

The Elks decided to award a ten-year lease of the theatre to Gus Sun.[386] Under the lease, Sun would provide three to four good, legitimate attractions a month and first-class vaudeville. Sun was obligated to furnish the theatre and to transfer the furnishings to the lodge at the end of the lease. He also agreed to share a percentage of any construction costs that exceeded \$35,000.[387]

Sun decided to name the theatre the Alhambra, after the name of the palace in Granada, rather than Elks Theatre.[388] It opened with the musical comedy *The Quaker Girl*, which had very successful runs in London and New York. Senator-elect Warren G. Harding, an Elk, opened the theatre with a speech.[389] The show had a large cast and crew of sixty people who traveled to Marion using six railway cars, made up of a day car, a dining car, two

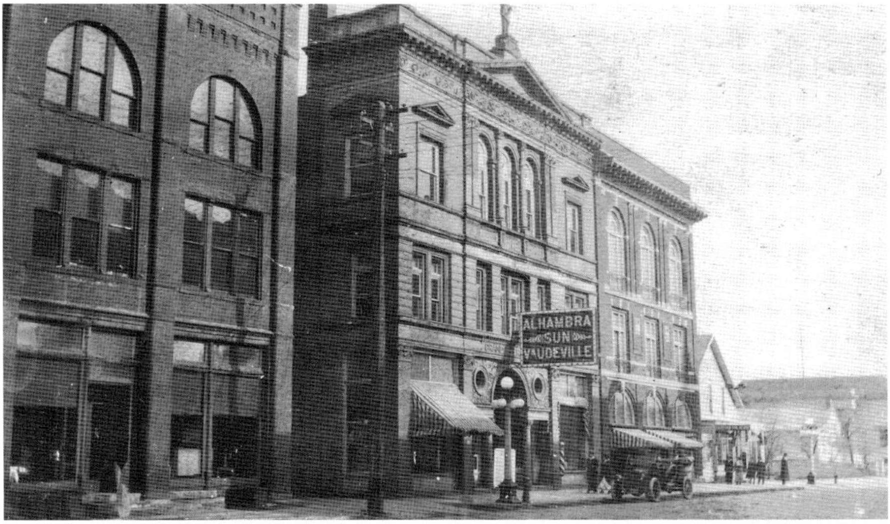

The Alhambra Theatre, rebuilt on the site of the Grand Opera House, circa 1915. *Courtesy of the Mike and Linda Perry Collection.*

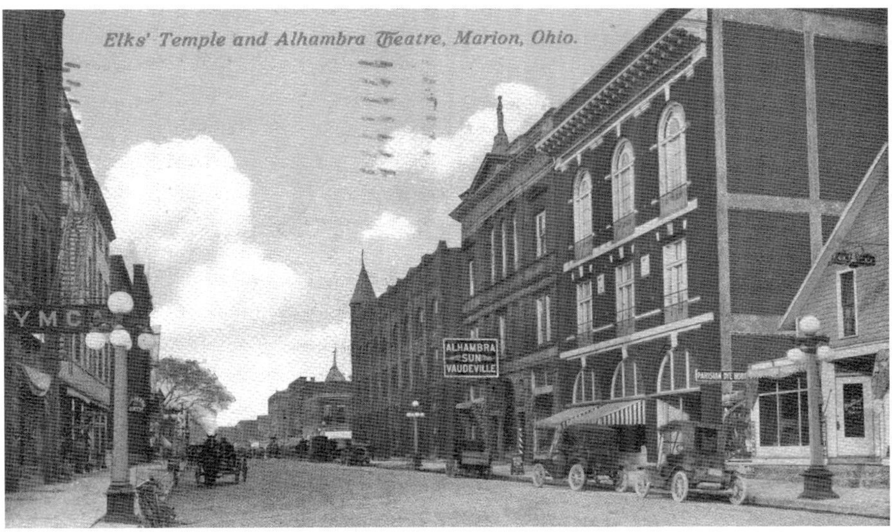

The rebuilt theatre was also called the Sun Theatre, circa 1915. Gus Sun leased the theatre from the local Elks lodge. *Courtesy of the Mike and Linda Perry Collection.*

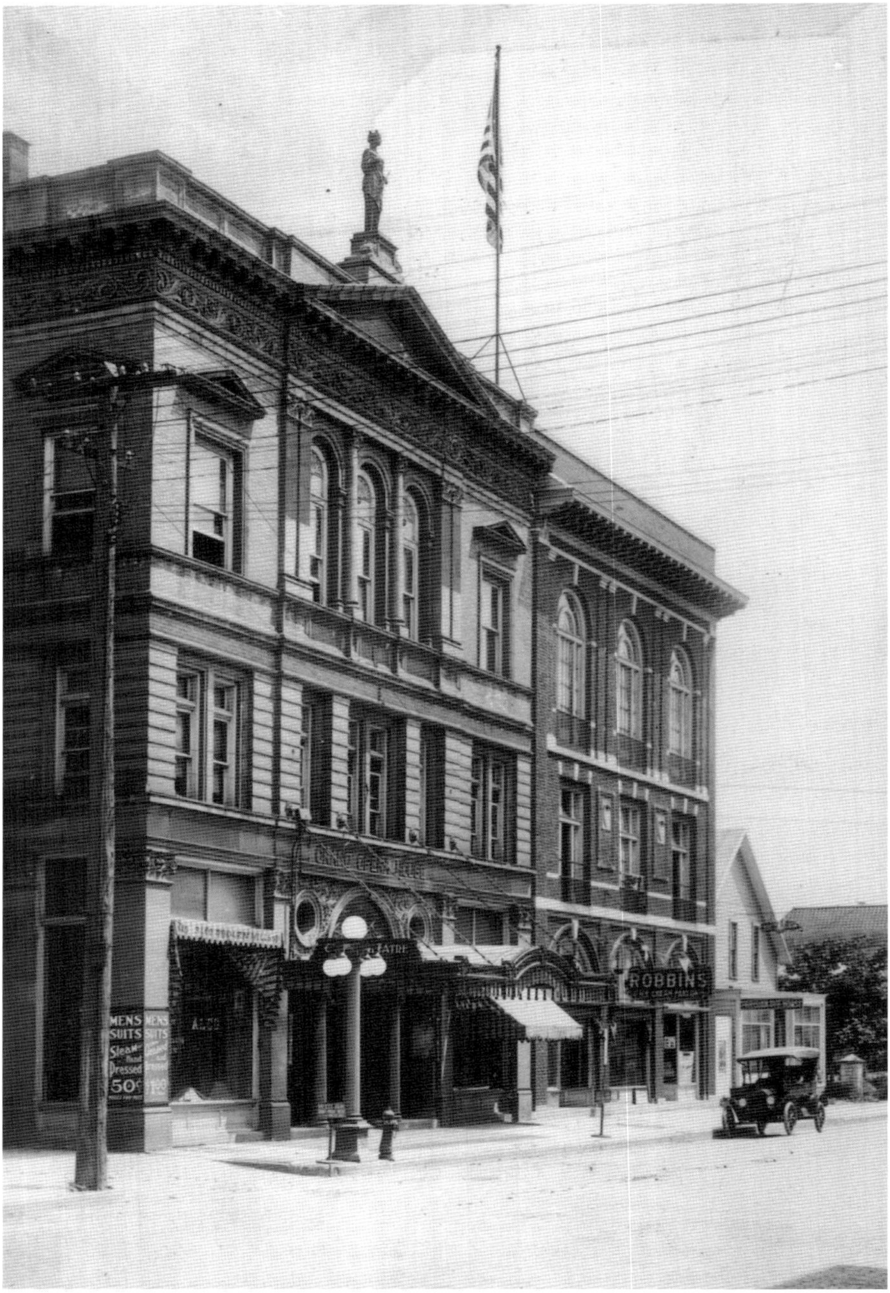

The Grand Theatre, circa 1916. After Gus Sun stopped managing the theatre, the name was changed to the Grand Theatre. A covered entrance was added to the building in 1916. *Courtesy of the Mike and Linda Perry Collection.*

sleeping cars and two sixty-foot baggage cars.[390] Proceeds from opening night, over $1,500, were donated to the Elks.

Operated as a vaudeville house, Sun changed the entertainment every Monday and Thursday. Evening performances were at 7:00 and 9:00 p.m., and matinees were at 2:30 p.m. When opened, ticket prices were ten, fifteen and twenty cents, with ten-cent tickets sold for the entire house at matinees. He also scheduled five legitimate (non-vaudeville) theatre productions a year.

The theatre stopped using the Alhambra name in 1916 and was renamed the Grand Theatre. A new covered entrance and signage were added. The lessee of the theatre after Gus Sun is not known, although the Elks produced many benefit shows at the theatre during the 1920s.

OHIO (1930–63)

The Grand Theatre became the Ohio Theatre on May 1, 1930, after a renovation.[391] It required extensive work, including installation of equipment for talkies. By August, one of the shareholders had asked the Marion Common Pleas Court to appoint a receiver to protect his interests.[392] The theatre was heavily in debt. In September 1930, the theatre operation was sold to John J. Huebner of Cincinnati.[393] In 1929, he had been the receiver for the financially troubled Marion Photoplay Co., which operated the Grand, Marion and Orpheum Theatres.[394] Huebner managed the theatre during the 1930s and '40s, until he sold it to Selected Theatres Co., a Cleveland company, in 1946.[395]

Selected Theatres completely renovated the Ohio before it reopened in 1949 as the "New Ohio." The street-level façade was remodeled with peach-colored columns and a new glass and aluminum marquee. The foyer, mezzanine and theatre were redecorated with dark green walls and fabrics and mahogany panels. A mural of the Harding Memorial was placed at the entry of the auditorium. Doors were decorated with green leather studded with nail heads. All new seats were installed, at a cost of $25,000. The theatre was ready for postwar entertainment.

The company operated the theatre until the one-thousand-seat Ohio closed its doors in August 1963. Ticket sales had plummeted due to the popularity of television.[396] It remains closed today.

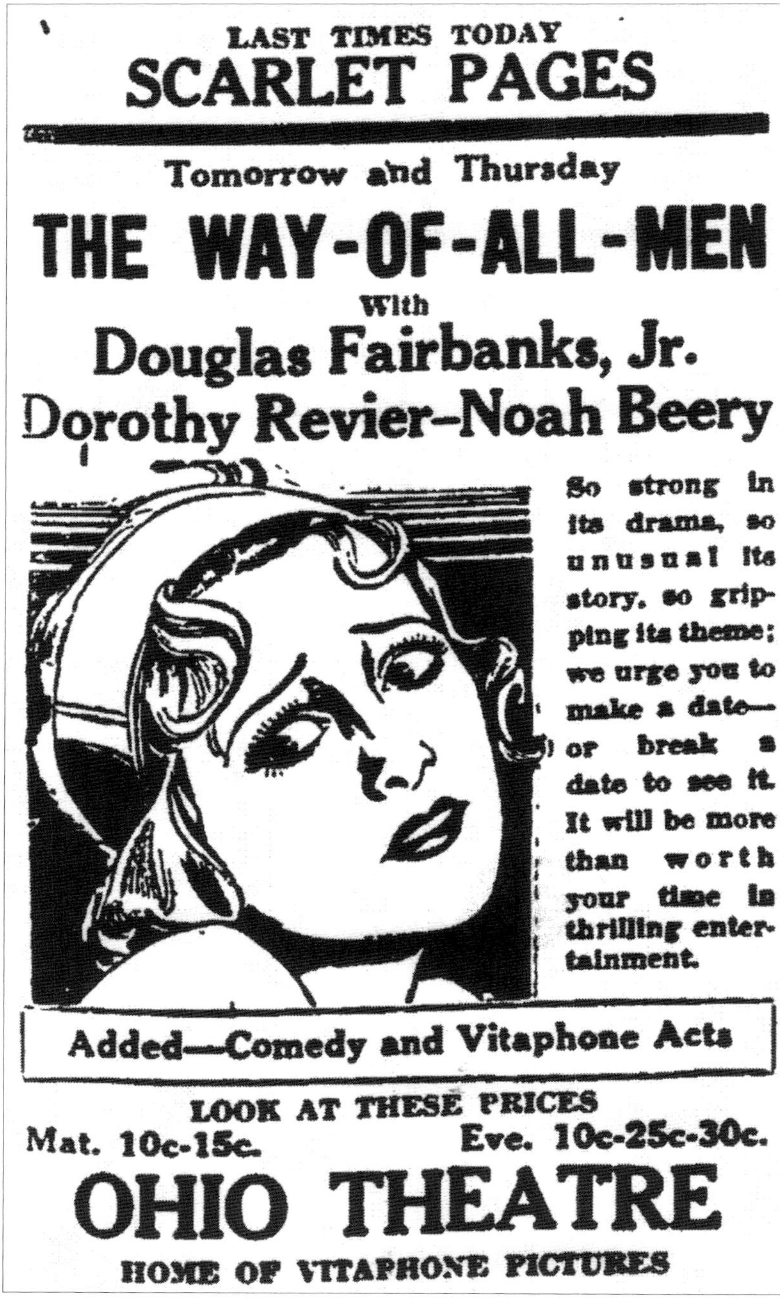

An October 7, 1930 *Marion Star* advertisement for the Ohio Theatre. *Courtesy of the* Marion Star.

NICKELODEON (1906–08)

The Nickelodeon, located at 124 South Main Street, opened during 1906. It showed moving pictures in a converted storefront for an admission charge of five cents. Less expensive than a vaudeville show, the Nickelodeon provided laborers with an inexpensive night of entertainment. It was a small theatre, seating no more than one hundred people, and showed short moving pictures that ran continuously. Seats were either wooden chairs or benches, and the building was poorly ventilated.

Throughout the country, these theatres were not well received. In addition to the primitive comforts, they developed a reputation among religious and civic groups for all sorts of actual and perceived threats to social order. Unlike later movie theatres with dim lighting, the Nickelodeon would have been almost completely dark inside. Some worried that this encouraged intimacy and promiscuity among young couples. Yet for the working class, particularly farmers and factory workers, the Nickelodeon was an affordable leisure activity.

The motion pictures exhibited at the Nickelodeon ran from ten minutes to an hour in length. They included comedy, melodrama, western, slapstick, history and social commentary. To ensure that patrons returned often, the theatre would change its program at least twice per week.

After paying the admission price, patrons could enter the theatre in the middle of a motion picture and stay as long as they liked. Most of the motion pictures were made in Chicago and rented to the Nickelodeon's owner. A piano player provided music to accompany the motion picture, and sometimes the audience would sing along while the lyrics were projected on the screen (called an "illustrated song").

On April 6, 1908, the Nickelodeon increased the adult admission price to ten cents and began to operate what it called a "vaudette" program.[397] Shows of one hour each now included a mix of entertainment, including soloists, dancers and a motion picture—clearly intended to compete for patrons of vaudeville theatres.

Financial problems resulted in a receiver being appointed in September 1908 to operate the theatre and pay its debts from the revenues.[398] The receiver also had problems operating the Nickelodeon at a profit, and it was closed in December 1908.[399]

CASINO (1909–10)

In August 1909, William Stansbury opened the Casino in the same location as the Nickelodeon. The Marion city directory lists the address as 128 (124) South Main Street, so Stansbury may have taken over the entire building rather than just the half used previously by the Nickelodeon. It was also operated as a nickelodeon, showing motion pictures. A soloist, Miss Darst, performed often. At the time, theatre managers struggled with providing sufficient comfort to patrons. In December 1909, the Casino advertised that it had one of the best floor heaters in Marion: "Room always cozy and warm."[400] It closed in mid-April 1910.

LUNA (1910–11)

In 1910, William Stansbury reopened the Casino as the Luna in the same location. It continued to operate as a nickelodeon, in the same manner as the Nickelodeon and the Casino. A typical bill featured two films, with a piano player or a small orchestra and a song performed by a soloist.

To differentiate itself from the other theatres, the Luna stressed safety. In a 1910 *Daily Mirror* advertisement, the Luna reassured patrons that its films were licensed at an extra cost to the theatre of two dollars each week.[401] Licensed films were considered to be fireproof and had the additional benefit of being reviewed by a New York censor.[402] If the censor found a film to be "loud or vulgar," it could not be licensed. The Luna also announced in the ad that it had taken steps to provide a sanitary, germ-free theatre. It installed a machine to spray the walls with formaldehyde, as a "guard against any spread of disease."[403] In addition to differentiating itself by claims of safety, the theatre management also tried to attract patrons by giving away free gifts.[404] Starting in June 1911, patrons were given coupons for attending a performance, which could be redeemed for silverware. Ten coupons could be redeemed for a teaspoon and fifteen for a fork.

The Luna stopped advertising in the summer of 1911. In December, the storefront used by the theatre became a saloon, owned by Herman Fendner and Mark Huggins.[405]

BIJOU/BIJOU DREAM (1907–12)

The Bijou Dream Theatre was located at 126 North Main Street, now part of the site of the county courthouse parking lot. It appears to have had several owners over its short history, including Robert Herkimer, J.C. Wise[406] and Arthur Brandebay. The Bijou and the Casino were both managed by E.L. Willis, until he disappeared in February 1909, leaving his wife with the theatres and owing about $1,000 in debts and unpaid wages.[407] At the time, Willis owned the Bijou Dream with Robert Herkimer, who had the largest financial interest. He took with him about $300, representing both theatres' receipts for the previous week.[408]

In June 1908, the state building inspector announced requirements for fire safety at the Bijou and other theatres in Marion.[409] The Bijou needed to have two doors that swung outside, marked "Exit" with a red light over each.[410] Also, the owner was instructed not to sell more tickets than the Bijou had the capacity to hold for safe fire evacuation.[411]

By early 1912, the finances of the Bijou had deteriorated, and the theatre closed.[412] The Bijou became a bar in February 1912, owned by Brook Club Distributing Company.[413]

LYRIC (1907–08)

The Lyric was a moving picture house located at 137½ North Main Street, which opened for business sometime in 1907. The Lyric was owned by Frank Conlan, until he sold to Eddie Anthoni on April 20, 1908.[414] Anthoni became somewhat of a celebrity in Marion when, on May 9, 1908, he assaulted Benjamin Bigford, a local constable, and literally threw him from the theatre to the street.[415] The poor constable, a small man, had attempted to take away the cash from the theatre under a court order. The money was then to be paid to a piano player who was owed for his performances. Constable Bigford subsequently arrested Anthoni for assault but missed the court appearance because of his injuries.[416]

The Lyric was the scene of an unintentional bulldog fight on a Saturday night in April 1908.[417] Mrs. Frank Bryan, wife of a North Main Street cigar and poolroom proprietor, had brought her bulldog to the show, not an unusual thing to do at the time. But panic erupted at about nine o'clock when another bulldog entered the crowded theatre and a dogfight ensued.

Patrons who could not escape jumped to their chairs as one dog chased the other around the room. It took ten minutes to break up the fight. The *Star* reported that some women were so excited that they had to leave the theatre to return home.[418] The theatre's reputation apparently became too much for Marion, and the Lyric closed in May 1908. It reopened as the Wonderland.

WONDERLAND (1908–15)

The Wonderland opened on August 1, 1908. The location was either at the former site of the Lyric (137½ North Main Street) or next door at 135 North Main Street; inconsistent information can be found in the historical records. The Wonderland was owned by Jonathan F. Redd. He installed an electrical production plant for the theatre that allowed him to show moving pictures even when the city's unpredictable power system was dark.[419] He

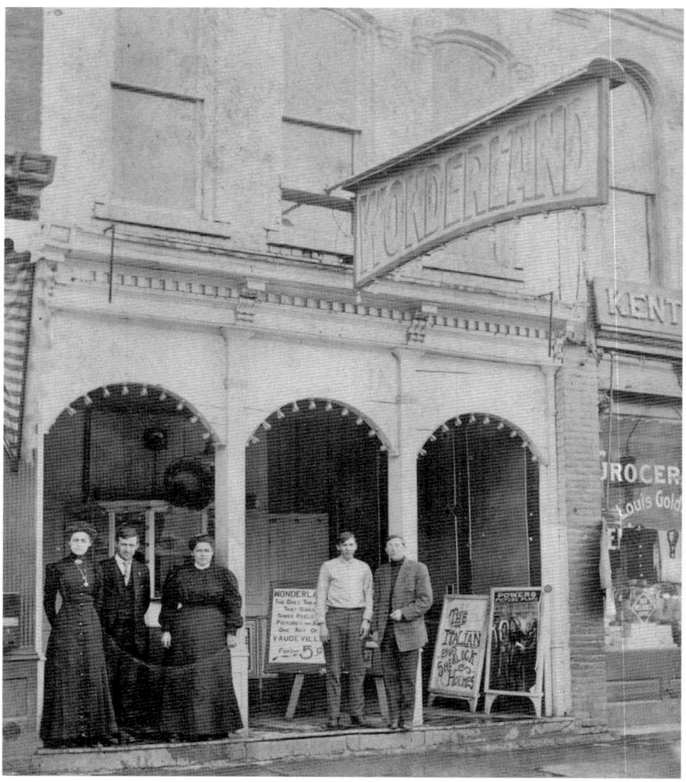

The Wonderland Theatre with its owners and employees, circa 1908–15. This photograph shows a sign advertising that the Wonderland is the only theatre that gives three rolls of film and a vaudeville act for only a nickel. *Courtesy of the Mike and Linda Perry Collection.*

also brought small vaudeville acts to the theatre. Redd sold the Wonderland on April 1, 1913, to G.A. Benz and J. Oesterle, who continued operations with the Wonderland name.[420] It was subsequently sold again in 1914 and stopped advertising after 1915.[421]

DREAMLAND (1906–08)

Dreamland also operated during the nickelodeon era. It was located at 136 East Center Street. The theatre ceased advertising in 1908. It is likely that it closed soon after the state building inspector visited Marion. He ordered numerous safety changes to schools, lodges, clubs and theatres. In a June 1, 1908 *Marion Daily Star* article, the order was described as "a big one."[422] The Dreamland, Bijou Dream, Lyric and Nickelodeon owners were ordered to install two exits with the doors swinging out and marked "Exit" with a red light installed above each door. It also required that the theatres limit ticket sales to their seating capacity and not sell standing-room tickets. The *Star* reported that the Bijou Dream and the Nickelodeon would comply with the order. The Lyric was closed when the order was issued. It was not known at the time of the article what the Dreamland would do, but given the absence of advertising after that order was issued, either the owners couldn't comply or decided they could not operate profitably under the order.

QUEEN THEATRE (1909–10)

Located at 208 East Center Street, the Queen Theatre was owned by M.A. Neff. He attempted to drive business to his motion picture theatre by partnering with local businesses. Patrons of the businesses would receive Queen Theatre tickets, based on their purchases at the local businesses. Once a patron had made a dollar's worth of purchases at any combination of several businesses, the coupons received could be exchanged for free admission to the Queen.[423] The concept was not a success, and the theatre was sold.

ROYAL THEATRE (1911-16)

The Queen Theatre was sold to George Sayre and reopened as the Royal.[424] Like most new owners of theatres, Sayre updated the décor.[425] Located across the street from the office of the *Marion Daily Star*, Nellie, the *Star*'s office dog, would sometimes cross East Center Street and watch motion pictures in the theatre. A July 24, 1913 article noted that Nellie attracted "considerable attention."[426]

In June 1914, the theatre was updated and remodeled, including the addition of electric fans and a new ventilation system.[427] The theatre was also equipped with new Edison motion picture projectors. It ceased advertising in 1916 and presumably closed soon after that.

MARION FAMILY THEATRE (1906-09)

The Marion Family Theatre was located at the southwest corner of West Center and Union Streets. In the 1910 Marion city directory, the address is listed as 247 West Center Street. The theatre opened in 1906 as a vaudeville house and competitor to the Grand Opera House.

The manager and lessee was H.S. Vail, who also operated theatres in Findlay and Delaware. In May 1908, Vail was reported missing and was presumed to have left town without paying performers or creditors. Charles E. Merkel, the owner of the building, foreclosed on a mortgage he held and took action to take the few assets that Vail left behind. As this would have left the performers penniless, Merkel and the sheriff agreed that the show would go on for two nights, with the receipts divided among the performers. The theatre then closed.[428]

A few days later, on May 30, 1908, Vail returned to pay off creditors. In a *Star* interview, Vail explained, "Business has been bad on account of the financial depression all over the country, and I have simply been caught."[429] Merkel allowed Vail to continue the lease, provided rent was prepaid each month. That plan worked until August 19, 1909, when Merkel closed the theatre due to unpaid rent.[430] Vail blamed late rent on an employee.[431] Merkel had been in discussions with other theatre operators and saw no reason to continue to work with Vail. It became the Orpheum in September, but it was also referred to as the "family theatre."

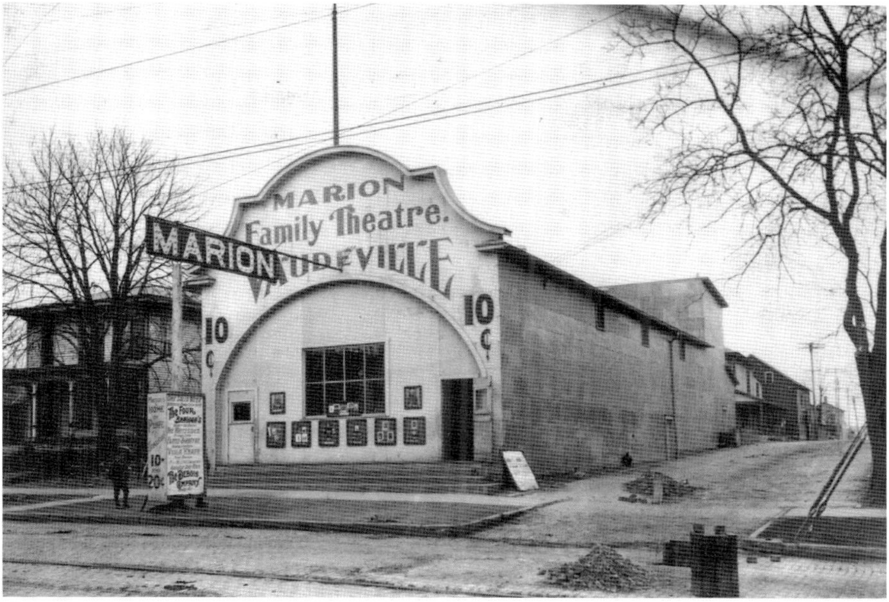

The Marion Family Theatre, circa 1906. Light bulbs surrounded the archway and outlined the name "Marion" on the hanging sign. It was located at the corner of Union and West Center Streets. *Courtesy of the Mike and Linda Perry Collection.*

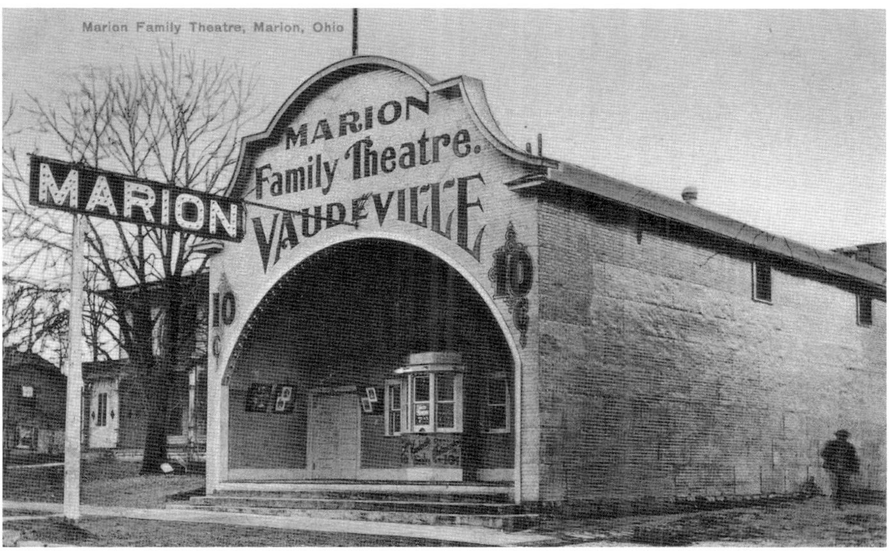

The Marion Family Theatre after a remodeling, circa 1909. The entrance was changed to provide a covered entrance and box office. Exit doors were widened to comply with stricter state fire regulations. *Courtesy of the Mike and Linda Perry Collection.*

ORPHEUM (1909–10)

Merkel announced on August 25, 1909, that the theatre was leased to the Sun-Murray vaudeville firm under a five-year lease.[432] It operated as a vaudeville theatre, this time with the booking strength of the Sun-Murray firm.[433] The theatre was marketed as the Orpheum, but the name "Sun Vaudeville" also appeared prominently. Sun-Murray controlled eight vaudeville houses in Ohio and Indiana and did the bookings (called a vaudeville circuit) for 126 theatres.

SUN THEATRE/SUN FAMILY THEATRE (1910–13)

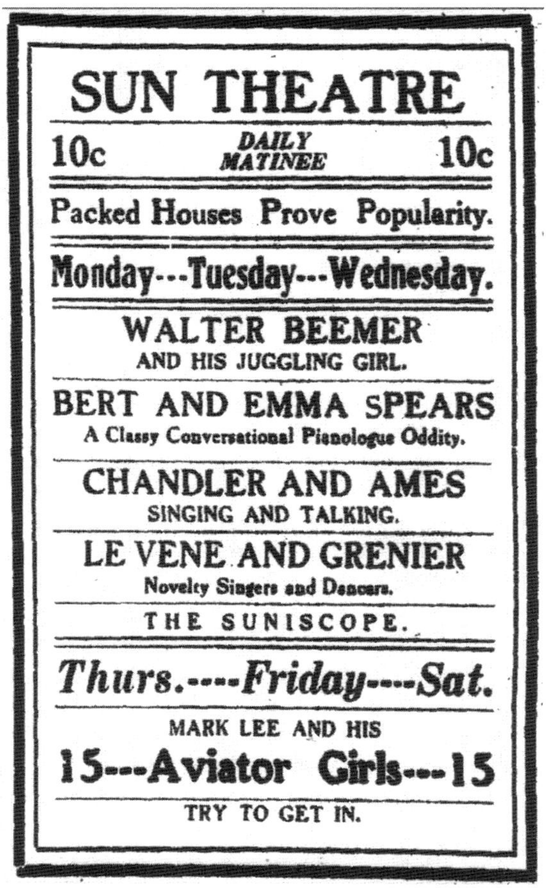

A November 18, 1911 *Marion Daily Star* advertisement for the Sun Theatre. *Courtesy of the* Marion Daily Star.

The name "Orpheum" had been dropped by December 1910, and the theatre was advertised as the Sun. It was still under lease to Sun-Murray. The Sun-Murray firm sometimes experienced difficulty in booking vaudeville acts that were acceptable to the different views of respectability found in the various communities where it operated. Marion mayor J.G. Seiter closed a performance of dancers on Valentine's Day 1911 because the costumes, or lack thereof, were inappropriate.[434]

Less than two weeks later, the Sun-Murray firm was no longer operating the theatre. Blepinger Brothers, a Dayton firm with theatres in Indiana and Ohio, took over as the operator.[435] However, the Sun-Murray firm continued to book vaudeville acts for the Sun. Despite the change in operators, the theatre remained popular in Marion. Even on Christmas Day 1911, every performance was sold out.[436] That day, the bill included vaudeville acts and motion pictures.

During the summer of 1911, the theatre was closed for renovations. A new façade, additional seating, renovated box seats and the addition of a gallery were among the improvements.[437] Once completed, the Sun had six hundred seats. During renovations, longtime theatre manager Fitzhugh Lee operated an Aerodrome on Prospect Street.[438] It was a large tent that seated one thousand people where vaudeville and motion pictures were exhibited until the Sun reopened in November.[439]

In January 1913, the Sun was closed. Manager W.D. Clark told the *Marion Daily Star* in a January 7 interview that the house wasn't large enough for the attendance necessary to support high-quality vaudeville.[440] Attendance had dropped at the once popular theatre because high-priced, quality talent could not be booked for a cost that could be supported by the ticket sales of a small house.[441]

FAMILY THEATRE (1913–15)

The theatre opened again under the Marion Family name in the fall of 1913, although it was often still referred to as the Sun Theatre. The manager, M.E. Hanley, a former vaudeville performer, was successful with bookings.[442] On September 15, 1913, a *Marion Daily Star* advertisement announced that six thousand people had attended the theatre the previous week.[443] In a minor renovation of the theatre in 1914, Hanley removed the front steps and replaced them with a ramp.[444] Operation of the theatre was again transferred in 1915.

THE CASTLE (1915)

In 1915, the Castle vaudeville theatre operated for a short time in the location formerly occupied by the Family Theatre. It gained some notoriety in Marion, more from its closing than its opening. The last song performed on the stage before it closed was "I Don't Suppose We'll Be Back Here Again for Months."

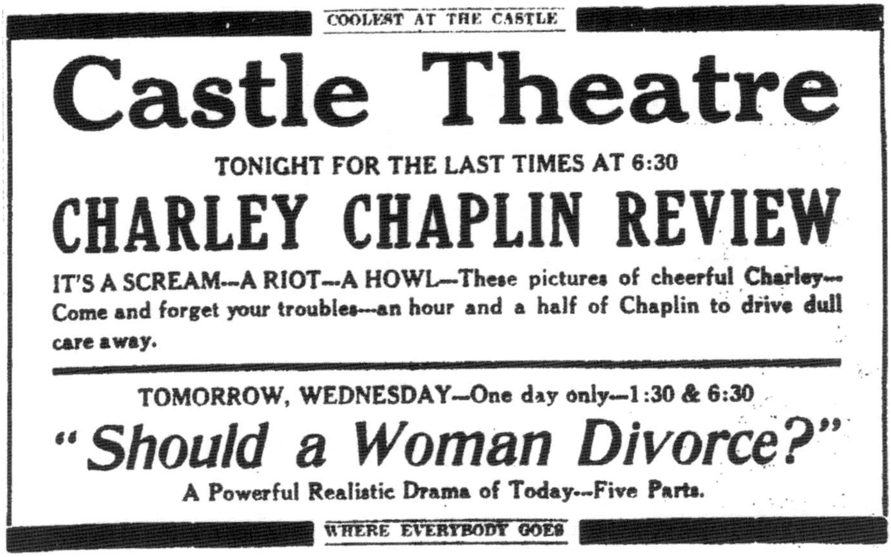

An August 17, 1915 *Marion Daily Star* advertisement for the Castle Theatre. *Courtesy of the* Marion Daily Star.

That tongue-in-cheek song, together with a note scrawled on a piece of pasteboard tacked to a dressing room door, alerted employees to the closing of the theatre. The note, written by C.A. Camplin, the manager, said, "Good-by [*sic*] boys. I hope you have better luck than I have had the last few months."[445] The landlord, employees and other creditors of the theatre were left scratching their heads. The *Marion Daily Star* reported that the financial troubles were attributed to a popular Christian evangelistic campaign in Marion, which caused attendance to drop. Camplin's trunks were seen loaded on an express wagon leaving the theatre. The last anyone saw of him was walking down West Center Street with two suitcases, presumably to catch a train.[446]

THE HART THEATRE (1915–19)

The Hart Theatre opened on November 8, 1915, at the same location as the Castle.[447] After the renumbering of Marion's addresses in 1917, the address changed to 219 West Center Street. The theatre was started by the Hart brothers, who formerly managed the Wonderland.[448] The Hart brothers managed a company of players formed in Marion that traveled throughout the country. At the time the theatre opened, the company had performed for fifteen weeks of drama and comedy at the Hart Theatre in Toledo.[449] The managers attracted national talent to Marion, including silent film star Eddie Polo and stage actress Myrtle DeLoy. The Hart Theatre closed in 1919.

NEW ORPHEUM (1919–31)

The New Orpheum opened on June 23, 1919, under the ownership of the Marion Photoplay Company, at the same location as the Hart Theatre. Edward Sharpless, a vaudeville star and Marionite, was the manager. Sharpless also managed the Marion Theatre. The opening program included three vaudeville acts and the film *The Source*, starring Wallace Reid.

Financial troubles began in 1928, resulting in several sales and reopenings. It was reopened on September 1, 1928, by George Iler and again on June 22, 1929, by George Maller. As the Great Depression began, Jack Raymond, the former pianist at the Grand, reopened the theatre as the Orpheum on September 3, 1930. He planned to exhibit motion pictures and small vaudeville acts. He died unexpectedly three weeks later, and his wife took over operations. The New Orpheum closed in 1931.

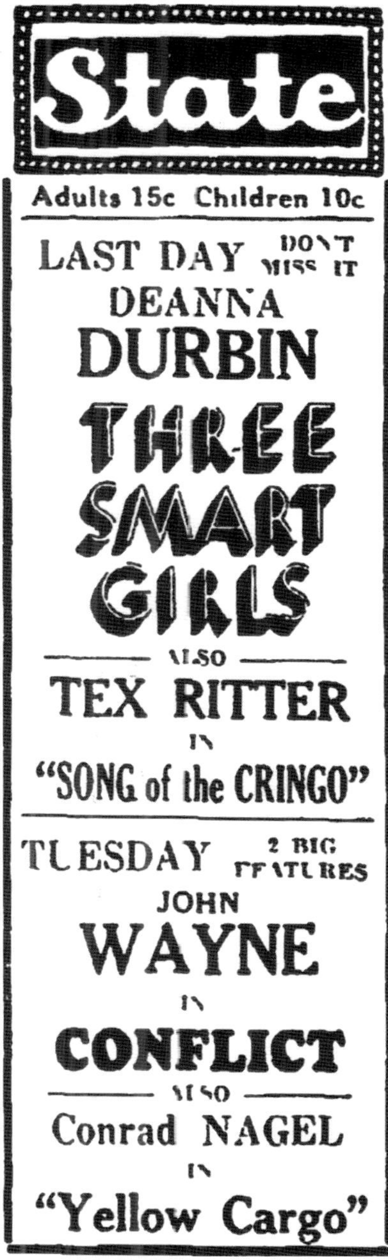

A May 17, 1937 *Marion Star* advertisement for the State Theatre. *Courtesy of the* Marion Star.

STATE (1931–57)

The State Theatre was located at 217 West Center Street on the site of the Marion Family Theatre. It opened in May 1931 and closed one month later for remodeling.[450] After remodeling, it opened again in September 1931.[451] The building was completely renovated in 1935, with new cushioned seats and a new sign and marquee.[452] During the 1940s, the theatre enjoyed popularity as a theatre that featured comedy films. Its bill included movies featuring Blondie, Abbot and Costello, Francis the Talking Mule, Tarzan and Shirley Temple. In 1957, the State Theatre closed.[453]

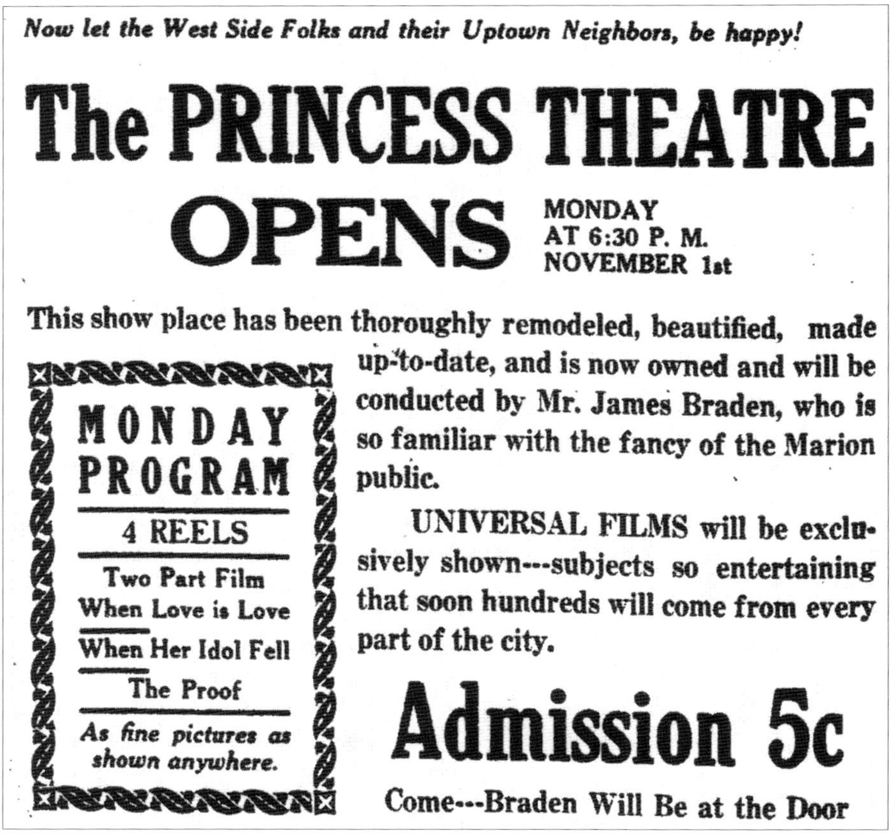

An October 30, 1915 *Marion Daily Star* advertisement for the Princess Theatre. *Courtesy of the* Marion Daily Star.

PRINCESS (1909?-35)

Located at 484 West Center Street (other addresses listed in the city directory are 592 [1915] and 486 [1934]), the Princess was opened as a movie house to cater to West End residents. It was the first theatre in Marion to exhibit a form of talking pictures in a very early use of that style of entertainment.[454] The Princess was also famous in Marion when the operator, Harry Longshore, was arrested on May 26, 1912, and fined twenty-five dollars for opening his theatre on a Sunday.[455] It became popular as the theatre for western movies. The Princess was closed sometime after 1934. At that time, the space was renovated for use as a grill and newsstand by H.L. Beach.[456]

MARION (1914-55)

The Marion was located at 170 West Center Street (the address was 247 West Center Street before the street renumbering in 1917), beside the Huber Building (also called the Uhler-Philips Department Store). At the time, it was also known as being located at the rear of the Concord Building.[457] Opened on October 20, 1914, as a photoplay house, the Marion had seven hundred seats.[458] The marquee was suspended over the sidewalk, decorated with copper, glass prisms and, according to the *Marion Daily Star*, one thousand "uncommonly brilliant" lights.[459] Over the marquee was a vertical sign, shaped like a bomb, with a bursting skyrocket effect displaying the word "Marion." Multicolored lights ran along the sign.[460]

The theatre was owned by the Marion Photoplay Company, whose principal investors were Edward Sharpless, G.H. Foster and Charles R. McMurray. Sharpless was a vaudeville ventriloquist star from Marion who appeared under the stage name of Ed Reynard (the "Great Reynard").[461]

Opening night invitations to the "Marion Theatre Beautiful" were sent to a list of prominent Marion citizens, including Warren G. Harding, Henry True, Frank A. Huber, Fred A. Stengel and C.J. Phelps.[462] The opening attraction for the public featured an organ concert by Clair Winston, the popular film star Clara Kimball Young in *My Official Wife* and a Broadway star feature provided by General Film Company. The film, which is now lost, was an enormous success and launched Clara Kimball Young and Earle Williams into first place in the popularity polls. Young appeared in person on the Palace stage in 1929, in a three-day run in which she starred in a vaudeville production.[463]

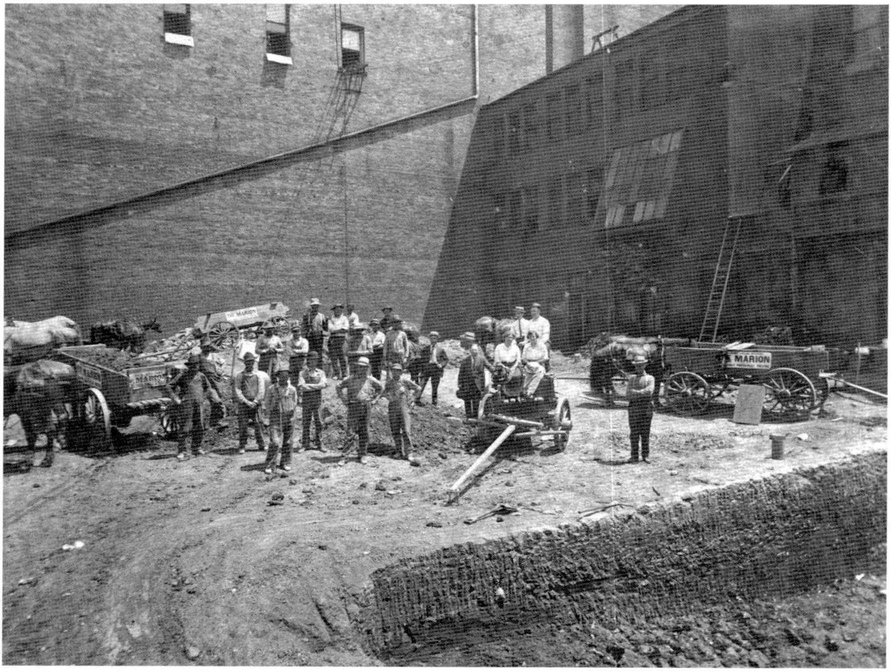

Excavation of the site for the Marion Theatre in 1914. *Courtesy of the Marion County Historical Society.*

The theatre was decorated in colors of ivory, gold, russet and green. Three chandeliers hung in the lobby. A large fifteen-foot arch led from the lobby to the auditorium. Seating was arranged in four sections, and there were nine slightly elevated boxes. The boxes, surrounded with brass rails, were furnished with bentwood cane-seated chairs and were carpeted. The aisles were carpeted with green runners to complement the green draperies in the boxes. Ivory-colored pilasters were installed through the length of the building. In the auditorium, six large, bowl-shaped light fixtures hung from the high ceiling, which could be used to create a variety of colors and lighting effects. The auditorium itself held a twenty-two-foot stage and an orchestra pit with an organ console. The stage itself was decorated with an old castle scene, with turrets and a castle wall. This moved to the sides when a film was projected. The stage was large enough for small cabaret entertainment but not large productions.[464]

Theatre fires were frequent and deadly in the early 1900s. The movie projector produced high heat, and the film was often highly flammable.

Consequently, at the Marion the projector was encased in steel, there were seven exits in addition to the main entrance and there were five fire hose pipes with fifty feet of hose each.[465]

The company equipped the theatre with several new innovations, including an automatic ticket machine, sanitary drinking fountains with coil-cooled water and a public telephone booth. A telephone system extended throughout the theatre, allowing communication with the organist, the stage, the projection booth, the ticket seller and the manager's office.[466] At a time when the audience would have to wait patiently while someone walked around the theatre to start or stop a film, this was a big improvement.

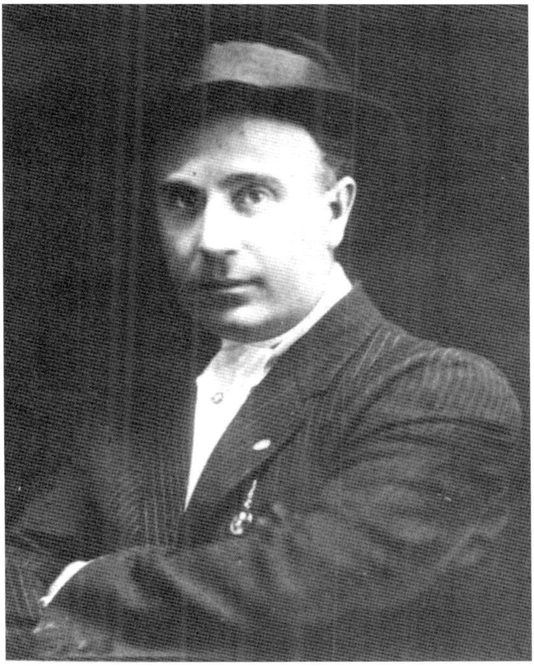

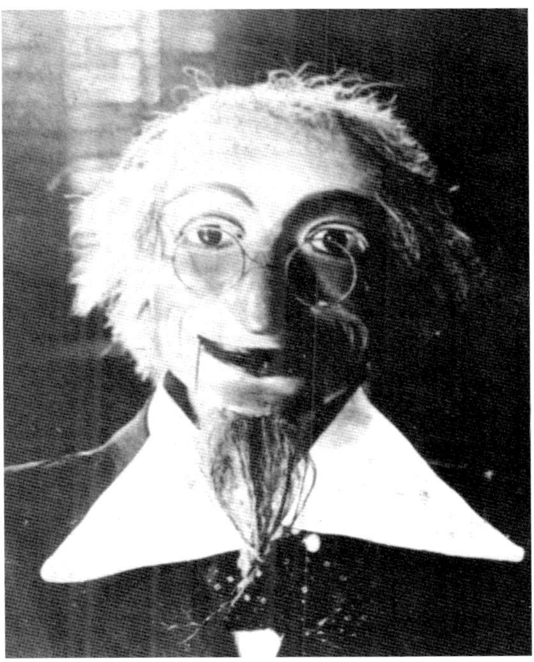

Top: Ed Sharpless, a co-owner of the Marion Theatre, was a nationally successful vaudeville star. A ventriloquist, his stage name was the "Great Reynard." *Courtesy of the Randy and Sandy Winland Collection.*

Right: Sharpless's routine was "A Morning in Hicksville," starring Judge Seth Dewberry, the Hicksville judge. Sharpless would also occasionally perform at the Marion Theatre. *Courtesy of the Randy and Sandy Winland Collection.*

The owners planned two matinees, at 2:00 and 3:30 p.m., and two evening performances, at 7:15 and 8:45 p.m. Admission was ten cents.[467]

Like other theatres in the city, the Marion closed during the Spanish flu pandemic (1918–20). The virus resulted in the deaths of about 3 percent of the world's population. On October 8, 1918, Marion theatres were ordered closed by the Board of Health. The order, in effect for two weeks, was an effort to stop the spread of the Spanish flu. Schools, lodges and churches were also ordered closed.

On October 18, 1928, less than two months after the Palace opened, John Huebner was appointed receiver to take over the Marion Photoplay

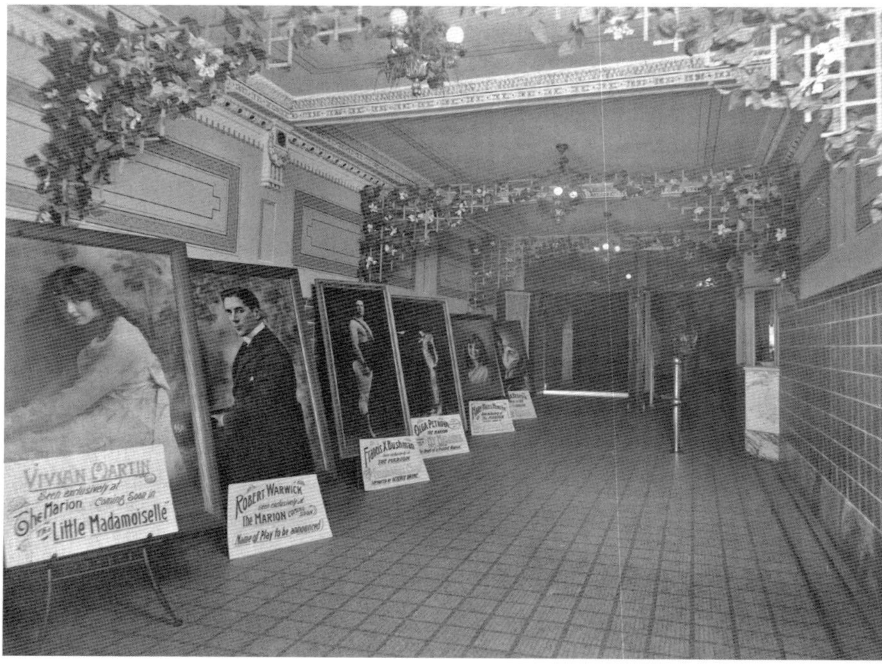

The Marion Theatre lobby in 1915. Large signs advertised upcoming performances. On October 21, 1915, Vivian Martin starred in *The Little Mademoiselle* (front left sign). *Courtesy of the Marion County Historical Society.*

Opposite, top: A Marion store window decorated to promote the 1924 Gloria Swanson film *The Hummingbird*. Also advertised were Hummingbird stockings. Customers who correctly guessed the weight of the suspended package won a prize. *Courtesy of the Marion County Historical Society.*

Opposite, bottom: The Marion Theatre entrance in 1925 with a promotional stunt for Richard Dix's silent film *The Lucky Devil*, a comedy about automobile racing. *Courtesy of the Marion County Historical Society.*

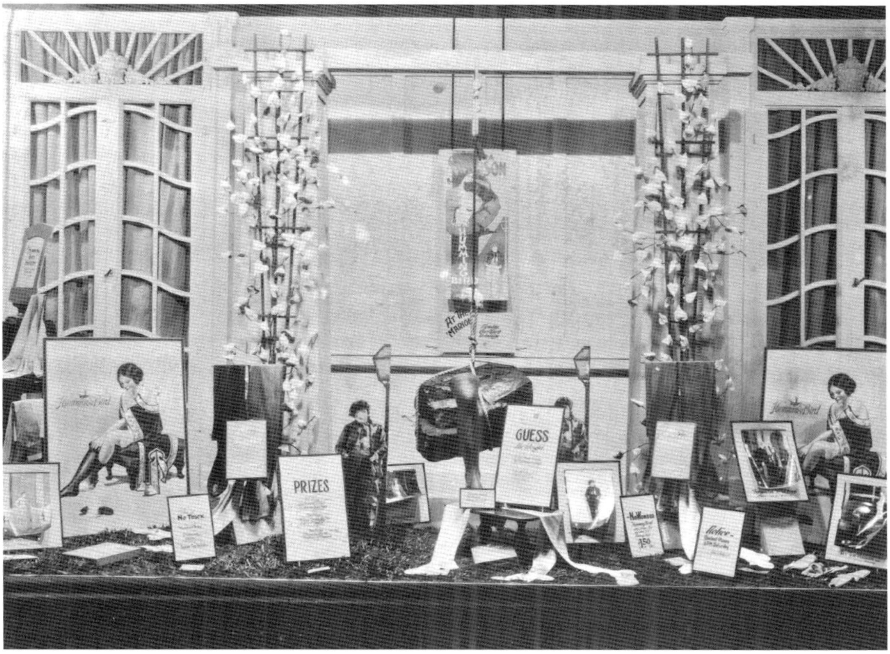
PRIZES
GUESS

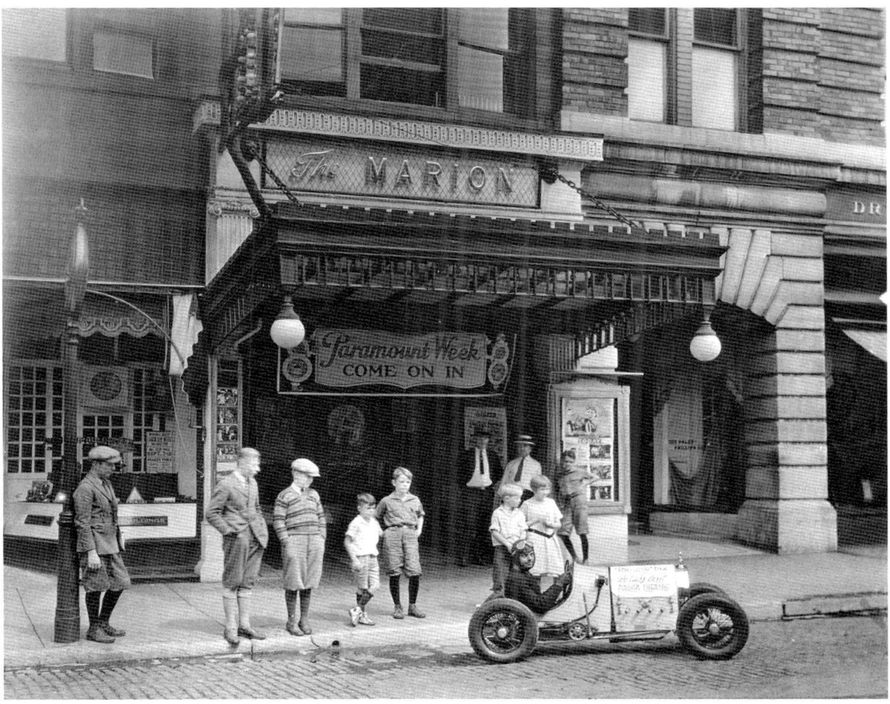
The MARION
Paramount Week
COME ON IN

Company, which could not pay its debts.[468] Marion Photoplay operated the Marion Theatre, the Grand and the Orpheum.[469] The Marion was closed to save financial resources, with plans to reopen it after the other two theatres were financially viable. Ten days later, the Marion reopened.[470]

In April 1929, the equipment of the Marion was sold to the Young Amusement Company, the operator of the Palace.[471] Young also took over the lease to the theatre.[472] In May 1929, it became obvious why Young had added the Marion to his list of theatres. Young had arranged a deal with Paramount-Lasky-Famous Players to operate the Marion and the Palace.[473] But not for long. Paramount, itself in financial difficulties, left Marion in 1932. Following that departure, both the Palace and the Marion were closed for seven weeks, until the V.U. Young Company reopened them.[474] In 1934, both theatres were leased to MidOhio Theaters Corp.

The Marion closed in 1955. Between 1947 and 1957, 90 percent of American households purchased televisions. With free programming available in the home, theatres attracted fewer and fewer patrons.

COLUMBIA (1910?–20)

The Columbia opened for business around 1910 as a picture house. It was located at 117 East Center Street. Following the 1917 street number adjustments, the address changed to 127 East Center Street. The theatre was often used by religious speakers and was a Marion County Chautauqua venue. The building was demolished in 1920 for an expansion of the Marion National Bank building.

REX (1916–22)

The Rex Theatre was located at 484 West Center Street. It advertised infrequently, and little is known about it.

OAKLAND (JOY) (1920?–50?)

The Oakland Theatre was located at 764 Davids Street, at the corner of Bellefontaine Street. It was opened in the early 1920s and completely remodeled in 1928, with new projection equipment, a new organ and all-female usherettes.[475] A receiver for the theatre was appointed in 1928, and the

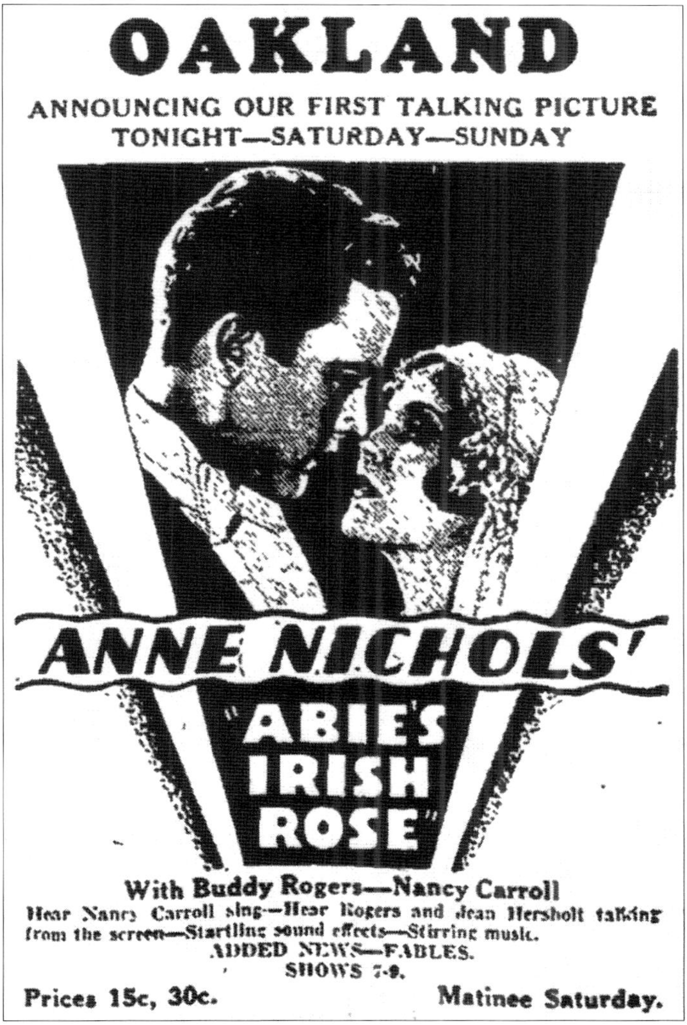

A July 19, 1929 *Marion Star* advertisement for the Oakland Theatre. *Courtesy of the* Marion Star.

theatre was sold.[476] It closed sometime in 1929 and was dark until April 12, 1936.[477] After reopening, it closed later in the decade and reopened under its nickname, the Oak, on February 29, 1940.[478] It closed soon after. On April 14, 1948, after a complete remodeling, it reopened again under new ownership, this time under the Joy Theatre name.[479] The remodeling of the 348-seat house included a new marquee, carpeting and updated restrooms.[480] The theatre closed for good in the early 1950s.

NOTES

INTRODUCTION

1. *Marion Star*, August 31, 1942, 11.
2. Marion County Recorder, Deed, vol. 502, p. 138.
3. Ibid., vol. 523, p. 485.

PART I

Chapter 1

4. *Motion Picture News*, January 7, 1928, 16.
5. *Marion Star*, July 19, 1927, 5.
6. Ibid., December 23, 1927, 1.
7. Ibid., August 29, 1928, 5.
8. Ibid.
9. Ibid., July 19, 1927, 1.
10. Ibid.
11. Ibid.
12. Ibid., 5.
13. Ibid., December 23, 1927, 1.
14. Ibid.
15. Ibid.
16. Ibid., 5.
17. Ibid.
18. Ibid.
19. Ibid.
20. Ibid.
21. Ibid., 1.

PART II

Chapter 2

22. *Marion Star*, August 21, 1928, 1.
23. Ibid.
24. Ibid., December 23, 1927, 1.
25. Ibid., August 29, 1928, 2.
26. Lane, *City of the Century*, 52; *Marion Star*, August 21, 1928, 1; August 29, 1928, 2.
27. Ibid., August 29, 1928, 6.
28. Ibid.
29. Ibid.
30. Ibid., June 22, 1928, 1; *Marion Star*, August 29, 1928, 6.
31. *Marion Star*, June 22, 1928, 5.
32. Ibid.
33. Ibid., August 29, 1928, 6.
34. Ibid., August 14, 1928, 1.
35. Ibid., August 25, 1928, 1.
36. Ibid., August 28, 1928, 5; August 25, 1928, 1.
37. Ibid., August 28, 1928, 5.
38. Ibid.
39. Ibid.
40. Ibid., August 29, 1928, 7.
41. Ibid., 6.
42. Ibid.
43. Ibid., August 21, 1928, 1.
44. Ibid.
45. Ibid., August 29, 1928, 6. Sindlinger was manager of the Palace for seven months before moving to Kokomo, Indiana, to manage a theatre there. Later, he joined *Time* magazine and managed the newsreel "March of Time." He later established a successful polling business and was an advisor to Herbert Hoover. He was the first pollster to develop a consumer confidence survey using skills he developed in surveying movie audiences.
46. *Marion Star*, August 29, 1928, 6.
47. Ibid., 5.
48. Ibid.
49. Ibid.
50. Ibid., August 24, 1928 (advertisement).
51. Hall, *Best Remaining Seats*, 163.
52. *Marion Star*, August 29, 1928, 7.
53. Ibid.
54. Ibid.
55. Ibid.
56. Ibid., December 23, 1927, 1.
57. Ibid., August 29, 1928, 2.
58. Ibid.

59. Ibid., August 30, 1928, 1.
60. Ibid.
61. Ibid.
62. Ibid., 5.
63. Ibid., August 31, 1928, 1.
64. Ibid.
65. Ibid.
66. Ibid.
67. Ibid., 1, 5.
68. Ibid., 5.
69. Ibid.
70. Ibid.
71. Interview with Drew Eberson, Theatre Historical Society of America Archives, January 1989.
72. *Marion Star*, August 29, 1928, 5.
73. Ibid.
74. Ibid.
75. Ibid.
76. Ibid., August 30, 1928, 1.
77. Ibid., August 31, 1928, 2.

PART III

Chapter 3

78. Griffen, *Westchester County*, 3:126; *Daily News* (Hamilton, OH), May 4, 1929, 2.
79. Klingaman, *1929*, 11.
80. John and Drew Eberson Architectural Records Archive Finding Aid, 4.
81. Ibid.
82. Ibid.
83. *Notable Men of Illinois*, 389.
84. Theatre Catalogue (1948–49), 3.
85. Rosenblum, *Boulevard of Dreams*, 128.
86. Ibid; Theatre Catalogue (1948–49), 3.
87. Rosenblum, *Boulevard of Dreams*, 128.
88. Ibid.
89. Theatre Catalogue (1948–49), 3.
90. John and Drew Eberson Architectural Records Archive Finding Aid, 4.
91. Theatre Catalogue (1948–49), 3.
92. John and Drew Eberson Architectural Records Archive Finding Aid, 4.
93. Levin, *John Eberson Scrapbook*, 2.
94. Eberson, "New Theatres for Old: Reconstruction," 930; John and Drew Eberson Architectural Records Archive Finding Aid, 4.
95. Levin, *John Eberson Scrapbook*, 2.
96. John and Drew Eberson Architectural Records Archive Finding Aid, 4.
97. Ibid.
98. Theatre Catalogue (1948–49), 3.

99. Levin, *John Eberson Scrapbook*, 2.
100. John and Drew Eberson Architectural Records Archive Finding Aid, 4.
101. Williams, "John Eberson," 572.
102. Ibid.
103. Ibid.
104. Ibid., 573.
105. John and Drew Eberson Architectural Records Archive Finding Aid, 4.
106. Ibid.
107. Ibid.
108. Ibid.
109. Ibid.
110. Hall, *Best Remaining Seats*, 95; Levin, *John Eberson Scrapbook*, 2–3.
111. Keim, *Our Movie Houses*, 76.
112. Levin, *John Eberson Scrapbook*, 2.
113. *Journal News* (Hamilton, OH), May 4, 1929, 2.
114. Levin, *John Eberson Scrapbook*, 2.
115. Ibid.
116. *Journal News* (Hamilton, OH), May 4, 1929, 2.
117. Hall, *Best Remaining Seats*, 96–97.
118. Ibid., 100.
119. Luna, "Those Enterprising Exuberant Ebersons," 26.
120. Rosenblum, *Boulevard of Dreams*, 129.
121. Elsa Eberson Kyle, Theatre Historical Society of America Archives, Comments of Elsa Eberson Kyle, daughter of John Eberson, n.d.
122. *Chicago Daily Tribune*, "Talkies Take John Eberson to Manhattan," July 21, 1929, B1.
123. Luna, "Those Enterprising Exuberant Ebersons," 26–30.
124. Eberson, "New Theatres for Old: Reconstruction."
125. Ibid.
126. John and Drew Eberson Architectural Records Archive Finding Aid, 5; Williams, "John Eberson," 576.
127. *Morning Herald* (Uniontown, PA), January 15, 1938, 7.
128. John and Drew Eberson Architectural Records Archive Finding Aid, 5.
129. Williams, "John Eberson," 576–78.
130. Ibid., 577.
131. Keim, *Our Movie Houses*, 76.
132. Williams, "John Eberson," 576.
133. Ibid., 577.
134. Ibid.
135. Ibid., 578.
136. John and Drew Eberson Architectural Records Archive Finding Aid, 5.
137. Schatz, *Boom and Bust*, 144.
138. Ibid.
139. *Billboard*, March 11, 1944, 3.
140. Ibid.

141. Valentine, *Show Starts on the Sidewalk*, 129.
142. John and Drew Eberson Architectural Records Archive Finding Aid, 5–6.
143. Keim, *Our Movie Houses*, 76.
144. John and Drew Eberson Architectural Records Archive Finding Aid, 6.
145. *Chicago Daily Tribune*, February 13, 1912, 6.
146. Ibid., August 16, 1911, 6.
147. Ibid., September 4, 1911, 2.
148. Ibid., October 29, 1911, 20.
149. Ibid., March 8, 1913, 1; July 8, 1913, 8.
150. Ibid., August 23, 1920, 1; August 25, 1920, 4.
151. Ibid., August 23, 1920, 1.
152. Ibid.
153. Striner, *Washington and Baltimore Art Deco*, 97.
154. Rosenblum, *Boulevard of Dreams*, 128.

Chapter 4

155. Preddy, *Temples of Illusion*.
156. Murphy, "Special Type of Motion Picture Theatre," 707.
157. Eberson, "New Theatres for Old."
158. Ibid.
159. Drew Eberson, "Foreword," *Theatre Historical Society of America Annual* (1975).
160. *Journal News* (Hamilton, OH), May 4, 1929, 2.
161. Williams, "John Eberson," 573.
162. Eberson, "New Theatres for Old."
163. Ibid.
164. Williams, "John Eberson," 573.
165. Ibid., 573–74.
166. Murphy, "Special Type of Motion Picture Theatre," 709.
167. Eberson, "New Theatres for Old."
168. Ibid.
169. Ibid.
170. Ibid.
171. Ibid.
172. Ibid.
173. Interview with Drew Eberson, Theatre Historical Society of America Archives, January 1989.
174. *Film Daily Yearbook* (1929), 932.
175. Interview with Drew Eberson, Theatre Historical Society of America Archives, January 1989.
176. Eberson, "New Theatres for Old."
177. Ibid.
178. Williams, "John Eberson," 574.
179. Ibid.
180. Eberson, "New Theatres for Old."
181. Hall, *Best Remaining Seats*, 100; Williams, "John Eberson," 573.
182. Eberson, "New Theatres for Old."

183. Hall, *Best Remaining* Seats, 100.
184. Eberson, "New Theatres for Old."
185. Ibid.
186. Williams, "John Eberson," 574.
187. Ibid.
188. Interview with Drew Eberson, Theatre Historical Society of America Archives, January 1989; Leccese, "Palace Guard," 3.
189. *Film Daily Yearbook* (1929), 930; Hall, *Best Remaining Seats*, 100.
190. Williams, "John Eberson," 575–76; Sharp, *Picture Palace*, 108, 160.
191. Williams, "John Eberson," 572.
192. Ibid., 576.
193. Hall, *Best Remaining Seats*, 93–94.
194. Ibid., 94.
195. Shand, *Modern Theatres and Cinemas*, 19.
196. Hall, *Best Remaining Seats*, 94.

PART IV

Chapter 5

197. Marion County Recorder, Deed, vol. 178, p. 263.
198. *Marion Star*, July 19, 1927, 1.
199. Ibid., 5.
200. Ibid., 1.
201. Ibid., December 23, 1927, 1.
202. Ibid., August 29, 1928, 5.
203. Ibid.
204. Ibid.
205. Ibid.
206. Ibid.
207. Ibid.
208. Ibid., July 19, 1927, 1.
209. Ibid.
210. Ibid.
211. Ibid., 5; August 29, 1928, 5.
212. Ibid., August 29, 1928, 5.
213. Ibid., September 12, 1930, 24.
214. Ibid., July 19, 1927, 5.
215. Interview with Drew Eberson, Theatre Historical Society of America Archives, January 1989.
216. *Marion Star*, October 31, 1927, 1.
217. Ibid.
218. Ibid.
219. Ibid., December 23, 1927, 1.
220. Ibid., October 31, 1927, 1.
221. Ibid.

222. Ibid.
223. Ibid., December 23, 1927, 1.
224. Ibid., 5.
225. Ibid.
226. Ibid., February 23, 1928, 14.
227. Ibid., March 8, 1928, 5.
228. Ibid., August 29, 1928, 7.
229. Ibid., 4.
230. Ibid.
231. Interview with Drew Eberson, Theatre Historical Society of America Archives, January 1989.
232. Ibid.
233. Ibid.

PART V

Chapter 7

234. *Marion Star*, August 29, 1928, 2.
235. Ibid., July 3, 1928, 3.
236. Ibid.; August 29, 1928, 6.
237. Ibid., July 3, 1928, 3.
238. Ibid., August 29, 1928, 4 (advertisement).
239. Ibid., 7 (advertisement).
240. Ibid., 6.
241. Ibid.
242. Ibid., August 28, 1928, 16.
243. Ibid., August 29, 1928, 6.
244. Ibid., August 25, 1928, 16.
245. Ibid.
246. Ibid.
247. Ibid.

Chapter 8

248. *Marion Star*, August 29, 1928, 7.
249. Ibid., 5 (advertisement).
250. Ibid., 7.
251. Ibid.
252. Hall, *Best Remaining Seats*, 179–95.
253. *Marion Star*, August 29, 1928, 8.
254. Ibid.
255. *Marion Star*, September 28, 1928, 15.
256. Ibid., October 5, 1928, 14.
257. Ibid.
258. Ibid.
259. Ibid., December 1, 1928, 12 (advertisement).
260. Ibid., January 1, 1930, 5 (advertisement).
261. Ibid., January 31, 1931, 5; October 3, 1932, 2.

262. Ibid., February 21, 1931, 8.
263. *Tuscaloosa News*, November 7, 1944, 3.
264. *Marion Star*, August 28, 1928, 5 (advertisement).
265. Ibid., August 29, 1928, 5.
266. Ibid., February 8, 1929, 1.
267. Ibid., February 5, 1929, 1; February 6, 1929, 1; March 7, 1929, 1.

Chapter 9

268. *Marion Star*, August 29, 1929, 5.
269. Ibid., 2.
270. Smith, *Popped Culture*, 119.
271. Ibid., 120.
272. Ibid.

Chapter 10

273. *Marion Star*, August 19, 1937, 1.
274. Ibid.
275. Ibid.
276. Ibid., 4
277. Ibid., 1.
278. Ibid., 4.
279. Ibid.
280. Ibid.
281. Ibid., 1.
282. Ibid.
283. Ibid., September 8, 1937, 1.
284. Ibid., 2; September 10, 1937, 5.
285. Ibid., August 19, 1937, 1.
286. Ibid., September 8, 1937, 1.
287. Ibid., September 9, 1937, 16.
288. Ibid., August 19, 1937, 1.
289. Ibid.
290. Ibid.
291. Ibid., September 10, 1937, 5.
292. Ibid., August 19, 1937, 4.
293. Ibid., September 10, 1937, 1.
294. Ibid.
295. Ibid., September 14, 1937, 1.
296. Ibid.

PART VI

Chapter 11

297. *Marion Star*, August 29, 1928, 2.
298. *Marion Daily Star*, December 8, 1906, 3.
299. *Marion Star,* May 17,1943, 2.
300. Ibid., September 5, 1936, 9; September 19, 1942, 2; July 9, 1914, 3 (Evans lot).

301. Ibid., November 11, 1880, 4.
302. Ibid., April 11, 1882, 4.
303. Ibid., September 16, 1900, 12.
304. Ibid., January 31, 1880, 4.
305. Ibid., March 14, 1880, 4.
306. Ibid., March 21, 1883, 4.
307. Ibid., April 11, 1914, 10.
308. Ibid., March 21, 1883, 4.
309. Ibid.
310. Ibid.
311. Ibid., May 28, 1883, 4.
312. Ibid.
313. Ibid., August 25, 1884, 4; August 29, 1883, 4.
314. Ibid., August 25, 1883, 4.
315. Ibid., April 11, 1914, 10.
316. Ibid., March 21, 1883, 4.
317. Ibid., June 28, 1893, 3.
318. Ibid., July 25, 1895, 8; July 26, 1895, 8; July 30, 1895, 5; October 7, 1895, 8.
319. Ibid., June 28, 1897, 4.
320. Ibid., June 26, 1897, 6.
321. Ibid.
322. Ibid., February 11, 1898, 5.
323. Ibid., April 15, 1902, 5.
324. Ibid., July 13, 1916, 6.
325. Ibid., October 25, 1877, 1.
326. Ibid., March 6, 1878, 1.
327. Ibid., April 5, 1878, 1.
328. Ibid., November 21, 1878, 8.
329. Ibid., December 2, 1878, 4.
330. Ibid.
331. Ibid., December 3, 1878, 4.
332. Ibid.
333. Ibid.
334. Ibid.
335. Ibid., June 8, 1880, 1.
336. Hall, *Warren G. Harding*, 45–52.
337. *Marion Daily Star*, February 19, 1889, 2.
338. Ibid.
339. Ibid., April 18, 1891, 4.
340. Ibid., April 28, 1892, 3.
341. Ibid., May 4, 1892, 2.
342. Ibid., March 9, 1895, 4.
343. Ibid.
344. Ibid., April 2, 1895, 5.
345. Ibid., August 20, 1896, 8.

346. Ibid.
347. Ibid.
348. *Marion Daily Star*, July 20, 1898, 4.
349. Ibid.
350. Ibid.
351. Ibid.
352. Ibid.
353. Ibid., April 2, 1906, 5.
354. Ibid.
355. Ibid., October 22, 1909, 5 (advertisement).
356. Ibid., January 23, 1906, 5.
357. Ibid.
358. Ibid.
359. Ibid., March 29, 1906, 7.
360. Ibid., December 6, 1910, 1.
361. Ibid., December 6, 1910, 6.
362. Ibid.
363. *Marion Daily Mirror*, December 6, 1910, 6; *Marion Daily Star*, December 6, 1910, 1.
364. *Marion Daily Star*, December 6, 1910, 1.
365. Ibid.
366. *Marion Daily Mirror*, December 6, 1910, 6.
367. *Marion Daily Star*, December 6, 1910, 1.
368. *Marion Daily Mirror*, December 6, 1910, 6.
369. *Marion Daily Star*, December 6, 1910, 5.
370. Ibid.
371. Ibid.
372. *Marion Daily Mirror*, December 6, 1910, 6.
373. *Marion Daily Star*, December 6, 1910, 5.
374. *Marion Daily Mirror*, December 6, 1910, 4.
375. *Marion Daily Star*, December 6, 1910, 1.
376. Ibid.
377. *Marion Daily Star*, December 7, 1910, 11.
378. Ibid., December 6, 1910, 1.
379. *Marion Daily Mirror*, December 6, 1910, 4.
380. *Marion Daily Star*, December 30, 1911, 5.
381. Ibid., September 8, 1913, 5.
382. Ibid., May 17, 1913, 7.
383. *Marion Daily Star*, August 8, 1913, 8.
384. Ibid., November 7, 1914, 4, 6.
385. Ibid.
386. Ibid., January 9, 1914, 10.
387. Ibid.
388. Ibid., October 1, 1914, 4.
389. Ibid., November 7, 1914, 4.
390. Ibid., November 2, 1914, 11.

391. Ibid., May 1, 1930, 5; March 28, 1930, 16.
392. Ibid., August 19, 1930, 2.
393. Ibid., August 19, 1930, 2; September 22, 1930, 1.
394. Ibid., September 22, 1930, 1.
395. Ibid., 1.
396. Ibid., March 30, 1963, 11.
397. Ibid., April 6, 1908, 5.
398. Ibid., December 28, 1908, 5.
399. Ibid.
400. Ibid., December 9, 1909, 12.
401. *Marion Daily Mirror*, May 18, 1910, 7.
402. Ibid.
403. Ibid.
404. *Marion Daily Star*, June 8, 1911, 11.
405. *Marion Daily Mirror*, December 23, 1911, 8.
406. *Marion Daily Star*, August 20, 1909, 5.
407. Ibid., February 8, 1909, 8.
408. Ibid.
409. Ibid., June 1, 1908, 9.
410. Ibid.
411. Ibid.
412. *Marion Daily Mirror*, November 20, 1911, 5; *Marion Daily Mirror*, February 15, 1912, 3.
413. *Marion Daily Star*, February 26, 1912, 5 (advertisement).
414. Ibid., April 20, 1908, 3.
415. Ibid., May 11, 1908, 8.
416. Ibid.
417. Ibid., April 27, 1908, 5.
418. Ibid.
419. Ibid., January 8, 1913, 5.
420. Ibid., March 22, 1913, 5.
421. Ibid., July 14, 1914, 4.
422. Ibid., June 1, 1908, 9.
423. Ibid., November 9, 1909, 7.
424. Ibid., February 16, 1911, 7.
425. Ibid.
426. Ibid., July 24, 1913, 3.
427. Ibid., June 17, 1914, 13 (advertisement).
428. Ibid., May 30, 1908, 8.
429. Ibid., June 1, 1908, 7.
430. Ibid., August 20, 1909, 3; August 23, 1909, 5.
431. Ibid., August 27, 1909, 7.
432. Ibid., August 25, 1909, 5.
433. Ibid.
434. Ibid., February 15, 1911, 3.
435. Ibid., February 23, 1911, 5.

436. Ibid., December 26, 1911, 8.
437. Ibid., May 27, 1911, 3.
438. Ibid.
439. Ibid., April 11, 1911, 12.
440. Ibid., January 7, 1913, 3.
441. Ibid.
442. Ibid., July 11, 1914, 7.
443. Ibid., September 15, 1913, 11.
444. Ibid., March 15, 1914, 14; July 11, 1914, 7.
445. Ibid., October 26, 1915, 13.
446. Ibid.
447. Ibid., November 3, 1915, 5.
448. Ibid.
449. Ibid.
450. Ibid., July 1, 1931, 5; June 4, 1931, 4.
451. Ibid., September 12, 1931, 2.
452. Ibid., August 28, 1935, 14; September 28, 1935, 14.
453. Ibid., March 30, 1963, 11.
454. Ibid., February 20, 1912, 12.
455. Ibid., May 27, 1912, 5.
456. Ibid., November 22, 1935, 2.
457. Ibid., October 17, 1914, 1.
458. Ibid.
459. Ibid.
460. Ibid.
461. *Marion Star*, September 4, 1937, 2.
462. Ibid.
463. Ibid., January 8, 1929, 10.
464. Ibid., October 17, 1914, 1.
465. Ibid.
466. Ibid.
467. Ibid.
468. Ibid., October 18, 1928, 1.
469. Ibid.
470. Ibid., October 27, 1928, 12.
471. Ibid., April 15, 1929, 1.
472. Ibid., April 12, 1929, 1; April 15, 1929, 1.
473. Ibid., May 15, 1929, 1.
474. Ibid., August 5, 1932, 4.
475. Ibid., June 28, 1928, 11.
476. Ibid., October 3 1928, 11.
477. Ibid., April 13, 1936, 1.
478. Ibid., February 29, 1940, 12.
479. Ibid., April 14, 1948, 10.
480. Ibid., April 2, 1948, 4.

BIBLIOGRAPHY

"The Akron Civic Theatre, Former Loew's Akron: John Eberson, Architect." *Marquee* 2, no. 2 (1979).

Bruno, Giuliana. *Atlas of Emotion: Journeys in Art, Architecture, and Film*. London: Verso, 2002.

Drowne, Kathleen Morgan, and Patrick Huber. *The 1920s*. Westport, CT: Greenwood, 2004.

Earl, John. "Landscape in the Theatre: Historical Perspective." *Landscape Research* 16, no. 1 (1991): 21–29.

Eberson, John. "New Theatres for Old." *Motion Picture News*, December 30, 1927.

———. "New Theatres for Old: Reconstruction and Re-Equipment Solve Problems of Overbuilding Orgy." *Film Daily Yearbook* (1929): 930–59.

Griffen, Ernest F. *Westchester County and Its People: A Record*. New York: Lewis Historical Publishing Company, 1946.

Hall, Ben M. *The Best Remaining Seats: The Golden Age of the Movie Palace*. New York: Bramhall House, 1961.

Hall, Sheryl Smart. *Warren G. Harding & the* Marion Daily Star*: How Newspapering Shaped a President*. Charleston, SC: The History Press, 2014.

Herzog, Charlotte. "The Movie Palace and the Theatrical Sources of Its Architectural Style." *Cinema Journal* (Spring 1981): 15–37.

John and Drew Eberson Architectural Records Archive Finding Aid, Miami Beach, FL. Wolfsonian, Florida International University, 2011.

"John Eberson Interview." *Daily Times* [Tampa, FL], October 15, 1926.

Keim, Norman O. *Our Movie Houses: A History of Film & Cinematic Innovation in Central New York*. Syracuse, NY: Syracuse University Press, 2008.

Kinerk, Michael D., and Dennis W. Wilhelm. "Dream Palaces: The Motion Picture Playhouse in the Sunshine State." *Journal of Decorative and Propaganda Arts* 23 (1998): 209–36.

Klingaman, William K. *1929: The Year of the Great Crash*. New York: Harper & Row, 1989.

Lane, James B. *City of the Century: A History of Gary, Indiana*. Bloomington: Indiana University Press, 1978.

Leccese, Michael. "The Palace Guard." *Preservation News*, February 1983.

Levin, Steve. "A John Eberson Scrapbook." *Theatre Historical Society of America* 27 (2000).

Luna, T.P. "Those Enterprising Exuberant Ebersons." *Marquee* 25, no. 1 (1991): 25–30.

Margolies, Edward, Charles Gwathmey and Harold Ramis. *Ticket to Paradise: American Movie Theaters and How We Had Fun*. Boston: Little, Brown, 1991.

Melnick, Ross, and Andreas Fuchs. *Cinema Treasures: A New Look at Classic Movie Theaters*. St. Paul, MN: MBI, 2004.

Morrison, Andrew Craig. *Theaters*. New York: W.W. Norton, 2006.

Murphy, E.C. "A Special Type of Motion Picture Theatre." *Pencil Points* (1928): 705–11.

Naylor, David. *American Picture Palaces: The Architecture of Fantasy*. New York: Van Nostrand Reinhold, 1981.

Notable Men of Illinois and Their State. Chicago: Chicago Daily Journal, 1912.

Preddy, Jane. *Palaces of Dreams: Working Drawings and Photographs: The Movie Theatres of John Eberson*. Exhibition catalog. San Antonio, TX: McNay Art Museum, 1989.

Preddy, Jane, and Richard Stapleford. *Temples of Illusion: The Atmospheric Theaters of John Eberson*. Exhibition catalogue. New York: Hunter College Leubsdorf Art Gallery, 1988.

Preddy, Jane, and Robert A.M. Stern. "Glitz, Glamour and Sparkle: The Deco Theatres of John Eberson." *Theatre Historical Society of America Annual* 16 (1989).

Rosenblum, Constance. *Boulevard of Dreams: Heady Times, Heartbreak, and Hope Along the Grand Concourse in the Bronx*. New York: New York University Press, 2011.

Schatz, Thomas. *Boom and Bust: American Cinema in the 1940s*. Oakland: University of California Press, 1999.

Sharp, Dennis. *The Picture Palace and Other Buildings for the Movies*. New York: F.A. Praeger, 1969.

Smith, Andrew F. *Popped Culture: A Social History of Popcorn in America*. Columbia: University of South Carolina Press, 1999.

Sponable, Earl I. "Historical Development of Sound Films." *Journal of the Society of Motion Picture Engineers* 48, no. 4 (1947).

Striner, Richard, and Melissa Blair. *Washington and Baltimore Art Deco: A Design History of Neighboring Cities*. Baltimore, MD: Johns Hopkins University Press, 2014.

Theatre Historical Society of America. "Loew's and United Artists State Theatre Louisville, Kentucky." *Theatre Historical Society of America* 21 (1994).

Valentine, Maggie. *The Show Starts on the Sidewalk: An Architectural History of the Movie Theatre, Starring S. Charles Lee*. New Haven, CT: Yale University Press, 1994.

Williams, Celeste M., and Dietmar E. Froehlich. "John Eberson and the Development of the Movie Theater: Fantasy and Escape." In *Contribution and Confusion: Architecture and the Influence of Other Fields of Inquiry*. Paper presented at 91st ACSA International Conference, Helsinki. Association of Collegiate Schools of Architecture, 2004.

Wondra, Keith. *From the Land of Andalusia to the Wheat Fields of Kansas: A History of Wichita's Historic Orpheum Theatre*. Charleston, SC: CreateSpace, 2011.